Golden Times

Golden Times

Burr Morse

ISBN 978-0-9818668-4-0

Editor-in-Chief: Steffen Parker
Design: Frederica Templeton, Mansfield/Templeton & Associates
Cover design: Bill Loring, Bromley Brook Design

Printed in the United States of America

September 2009

This book is dedicated to Betsy, the love of my life…
without Betsy there would be no golden times.

CONTENTS

Part Three
Sour & Sweet

Part Four
Miracle of Music

Acknowledgments

First of all I thank my wife, best friend, and world's most giving person, Betsy Parker Morse. I run every word I write past Betsy...those she approves of have now become two books...those she doesn't start great fires. Second, I thank my two wonderful sons, Robinson Cole Morse and Thomas Parker Morse...they're both destined for great things! I thank my brothers and sister, Punk, Tick and Susie...I know our parents are proud. I thank my editor-in-chief Steffen Parker, who may not sit down till 2 a.m. to sort out my latest literary mess. I thank Peter Campbell-Copp at Historical Pages Company for the publishing, Frederica Templeton for copyediting and graphic design, Ben Ghobadi for the printing, Bill Loring and Mike Ahearn for the cover design, and my cousin David Aiken for always carrying a camera and knowing how to use it. I thank all my friends in the fields of farming, faith and music. I'm forever grateful to my hardworking, loving staff at the Morse Farm and everyone who ever gave me an idea or told me a story. Lastly, I thank all the farm machinery that ever broke, evaporator pans that ever scorched, cows that ever kicked, and all else that has left me cussin' and carryin' on...that stuff builds fortitude... and gives me something to write about.

Prologue

I've been writing newspaper columns since my book, *Sweet Days & Beyond,* was published in 2005 and heard some discourse that a second book might be in order. Since the first book has been so good to me, or at least the folks who read it have, I've been thinking along those lines myself, and here it is: *Golden Times.* This book will mainly serve as a vehicle for those new stories to cruise along through our Vermont countryside.

To get started, I've written four special openers…yarns that'll help you better know who I am. There's always a little discrepancy between the pen and the personality. Usually my writing is free of war, politics, pestilence and pesticides, but that pleasant, organic feeling I create for my columns is not necessarily the real "me"…I started my life a surly little cuss and you deserve to know me 100 percent! My roots go back over 200 years in this bony, Vermont soil and my memory has seen fifty-five of them. Sit back. Enjoy yourself. Let me be four again and that surly little cuss.

THE SOUR AND THE SWEET

A round-faced toddler cowered behind an old Glenwood kitchen stove at the Robinson homestead in Maple Corner, Vermont. He peered out at a rotund, middle-aged man who stooped low to the floor and peered back. The man spoke, kindly, in a foreign accent.

"Good day, young man. How are you today?" he asked.

"Awful!" spit the boy.

"Do you like your sister, Susie?"

"I hate her!"

"You surely must be friends with that kitty cat?"

"No!"

"Your mommy and daddy?"

"I hate them!"

The rest of the conversation faded from the boy's memory along with other memories of the 100-year old farmhouse where it happened. That boy was me and the man was Dr. Hans Peter Laqueur, a psychiatrist from New York City. The conversation was my first memory. GOOD GOD, with a start like that I should have become a PSYCHOPATH!

That was 1952 and this is 2007. I sit here pounding out my second book. Our black dog, Averill, lies nearby on a rug in front of the wood stove.

The fire feels wonderful on this crisp winter morning. Our home sits at the edge of the woods, carved thirty years ago, with my own hands, from the surrounding timber. My good wife, Betsy, writes nearby and I have just asked her advice on my progress so far. "I didn't really like the word 'psychopath,'" she said. "It sounds a bit harsh. Why don't you look it up?"

I ask Merriam-Webster Online: p-s-y-c-h-o-p-a-t-h

Psychopath: a mentally ill or unstable person; especially: a person affected with anti-social personality disorder.

"It fits, honey," I holler, finding it hard to concentrate. The window to my left reveals a picture-perfect day with happy skiers heading out on the twenty-five kilometers of groomed cross-country ski trails that cover our farm. I've been on this place ever since we left the Robinson Homestead when I was just five. Betsy and I have raised two wonderful boys here, Robinson and Thomas, who are both great musicians and craftsmen. In spite of my beginnings, I'm the luckiest guy in the world. So how, putting it in Vermont lingo, did I get from theyah to heah? The answer lay buried for years in the fog of farming and raising a family, two things I never really felt competent at. The answer has only recently emerged and now comes alive again as I turn toward the window and gaze at those skiers.

And like the skiers, I had a lot of slippin' and fallin' to do before I learned how. The uphill slopes were wicked hard work and those heading downhill scared the hell out of me. With persistence though, (notice I didn't say patience) I've reached a full and graceful glide on the eve of my fifty-ninth birthday. My trail sits perfectly groomed under a bright, blue sky and my skis these days are fast, waxed by things like hard work, honesty, good luck, and, most important, faith. That's right…I believe that faith in God is the one thing that made me a whole person and has brought me to this great place today. I'm also thankful for a few key relationships in my life, my music, and, of course, my God-given ability to write things down on paper.

Dr. Laqueur really wasn't my shrink; no, four year olds didn't have their own shrinks back in those days, at least not in Vermont, they didn't. He and his wife, Ria had recently joined our town's growing population of summer people with their acquisition of the Vilbrine place just up the road from our farm. They first appeared in the spring of 1950. Their Ford Woody was packed full with luggage and furnishings for their Vermont home. The road leading to their house was a mixture of mud and snow. The Laqueurs stopped at our house, introduced themselves, and asked my father if he thought they should try the road.

"Only if you wanta get stuck," Daddy responded, breaking the ice.

He went and started up our Allis Chalmers C tractor and hitched it to the

Woody. The road was steep and Dad asked Dr. Laqueur, a portly man, to climb onto the tractor's front end to keep it from rearing up. Ria, a small woman, took her place behind the steering wheel of the Woody. With considerable effort, Harry Morse pulled Peter and Ria Laqueur to their summer home in Vermont and a long and lasting relationship between two families began.

Peter Laqueur had come to Manhattan from Holland by way of Argentina, where he and his first wife had gone to escape capture by the Germans. There couldn't have been a more diverse combination; the Morses, simple farmers who had hardly ever left the hills of Vermont and the Laqueurs, sophisticated Europeans. The relationship, however, quickly melded the superior qualities of Vermont maple syrup and sweet Sauvignon Blanc. The two families were to be friends for life.

My first meeting with Doctor Laqueur could have been a harbinger of things to come but it wasn't, thank God! I've always felt that we Morses gained a level of sophistication that we would not otherwise have had through our relationship with the Laqueurs. I remember cookouts up at their place where the steaks were as thick as family Bibles and the wine flowed liberally among the adults, foreign stuff for a family of native Vermonters. They even coaxed us clear to Manhattan a couple of times to visit them in their 5th Avenue apartment.

I remember during one such visit traveling around and around the Empire State Building in our '55 Plymouth, looking for a place to park. I had to pee and my mother, desperate for a solution, offered me a Howard Johnson cup. I filled it up and when I threw it out the front window, it returned through the back window, right in the face of my big brother! We finally found a parking spot and went up to the Laqueurs' lavish apartment where they served us rare roast beef. My older siblings and I had never seen that before so we got rid of it by stuffing our pockets full and pressing some, like gum, to the bottom of the table...for us, meat was meant to be cooked! Wouldn't it be nice if differences between people were always as simple and solvable as rare vs. well done? Maybe it could be with a little "psychology" and a tug or two from a friendly farmer's tractor.

GROWIN' UP

Dot and Harry Morse were madly in love with each other from the moment a shy Dorothy Aiken, the new teacher in Maple Corner, served Harry Morse an extra helping of succotash at a Maple Corner community dinner. She had just graduated from Keene (New Hampshire) Normal School, a hop, skip, and jump from the southern Vermont town of Putney, where her family's roots went back to the mid 1700s. His central Vermont roots were almost as deep. From the moment he finished cleanin' up his plate, Harry Morse courted Dot as their romance blossomed into a sixty-year marriage filled with happiness and charm. My siblings, Elliott, Sherwood and Susan, are ten, seven and three years older than me, respectively. I've always felt like an afterthought, but my parents lovingly referred to me as their "rowan crop." The rowan crop is a farmer's second cutting of hay which is both shorter and stubbier but sweeter and more nutritious. Wow, such propitious words they would be, if only the second part were true!

Elliott and Sherwood (who, thanks to our parents' creativity with nick-names, would become "Punk" and "Tick"), were so much older that I never felt I knew them as brothers. Susie and I, however, grew up close to-gether and fought like siblings. One time she convinced me to try sampling some cow poop…said it tasted like candy. I did. It didn't! For some reason, Susie never got a nickname like Punk, Tick or Burr, but I sure came up with some doozies!

When I was five, we moved from Maple Corner down to Grandpa and Grandma Morse's new farm on the County Road in East Montpelier. Grandpa Morse had built a home for our family and my father took over the management of the new operation. There were four bedrooms in our house, one for our parents and one for each of the three older children. I, the afterthought, slept in a hallway between Punk's and Tick's room on a roll-a-way bed. The fifth year of my life marked certain important milestones: that physical move, my beginnings as a farm laborer, and the knowledge that I was deeply allergic to hay dust.

I dreaded going to the barn because of that hay fever but had to, seven days a week. It started with itchy eyes, runny nose, and finally settled into my lungs with an obnoxious, asthmatic rasp. At night, back in my hallway, sleeping was sometimes difficult with the barrage of artillery being thrown at me from both of the big boys' rooms; Punk and Tick were not always kind about my snuffling. Although we're all good friends now, there were periods of my life where being baby of the family felt like a life sentence in a snot factory. I was paroled when I was sixteen as Punk, Tick and Susie all got married within a few months of each other. Suddenly I had my pick of three big beautiful rooms!

They all went off to jobs away from the farm and, in spite of my hay fever and terrible attitude, I agreed to stay and help my father. He sold the dairy cows in 1966 and started eking out a living with vegetables, beef cows, and maple sugaring. That same year I went off to the University of Vermont to study plant and soil science. It was my father's plan that I become the expert at the Morse Farm, but shades of the Glenwood came rolling back in spades. I hated what I was studying but somehow managed to escape there four years later with a B.S. degree. To this day, you could put what I know about plant and soil science in a half-pint berry basket and still have room at the bottom for rocks to make it look fuller!

I spent the best part of the next twenty years pulling weeds on this place. The soil on the Morse Farm packs down hard as concrete but somehow also holds water like a sponge. Many years, our vegetable crops succumbed to weeds, water, or both, while an ironic little drought took place in my love life...who, I thought, would be interested in a round-faced guy who worked seven days a week and made no money? Finally, at the ripe age of twenty-six, an angel named Betsy found me. Betsy Parker's brother, Chuck, had been one of my best friends throughout high school and college, and Betsy and I finally ended up together (Chuck has always said that happened because nobody else would have either of us).

Betsy, the angel, was willing to put up with my work situation and the meager cabin I had built in the woods up above our farm store. We settled into life as a couple quickly; some say too quickly as we were among the pioneers of a trend which is tragically too common here in 2007...living together without being married. More than once, Betsy recalls, my mother would have to answer some customer's question about the recently strung clothesline up at the cabin at the edge of the woods. One time Betsy was working close by and my wonderfully accepting mother replied: "Oh yes...Burr is shacking up and this is Betsy, the lovely girl he's shacking up with."

We were finally married by a justice of the peace in our cabin on March 19, 1977. Typically negative, I remember secretly giving our union only a "few months" at the very moment I said "I do." Shortly after our wedding, we started cutting trees around the cabin to let the sunshine in and enlarging it to accommodate the birth of Robinson Cole Morse in 1978 and Thomas Parker Morse two years after that. My family, the three people who I love more than life itself, served as catalysts for the beginning of my climb out of the doldrums.

THE FLAME WITHIN

Faith is the kingpin of my life, probably because it serves as a bridge to my next life, which I expect to be even better. I remember first understanding God when I was about eight. I was at Vacation Bible School over at the Old Meeting House, a vintage church built in 1823 which stands just a mile east of our farm. One of the teachers was blind and I had made fun of him to a group of kids during a break. A skinny girl came up to me afterward and suggested I was probably going to Hell. I made some crack about how it "couldn't be much worse than listening to her whiney voice." Soon after that, the teacher suggested we ask Jesus to come into our hearts. I don't know if the girl's scolding contributed to my decision or not, but I gave it a try. It was much more subtle than getting zapped by an electric fence and there were no fireworks, but I felt an immediate change. Since then every time I feel close to the edge, there's a certain presence that reins me in and lets me know everything is okay. Thank you, God.

A few years ago a casual friend of Betsy's and mine, Martha Holden, asked if I wanted to be part of a new prayer group she was starting up. I had shared with her some of the frailties in my life and she sensed that I could use a booster shot. Since no one else was interested, the prayer group became just her and me with blessings from my wife Betsy, the angel.

Since that time, I have been going up to Martha's house two mornings a week for some informal chatter, followed by each of us offering our cares and concerns up to God. In spite of worrying about what the neighbors think, I've found these years in our prayer group of two...no, Three...to have opened my life in ways I never would have imagined!

MUSIC'S MIRACLE

For some reason I was destined to be a trombone player. I remember riding to school with my mother one day when I was nine in our '59 Chevrolet. I'd never even touched a trombone, but there I was working an imaginary slide to the tune that was playing on the radio. Guess it made an impression, because shortly after that the Ellis Music guy came to hand out our rental instruments and I got, you guessed it, a trombone.

I hadn't asked for it and knowing what I know now, fifty years later, sure wish I'd picked out a jazzier instrument. I mean, trying to fit into a jazz niche with a trombone is like a skunk going to a dinner party and somehow expecting to feel welcome, but I opened the thing up. The Ellis Music guy pointed out a few things, showed me which end to blow on, and sent me home.

I've often wondered how anyone can become a trombone player. Slides on student model trombones are about as smooth as poorly working tire pumps and there's nothing as annoying, knowing what I do today, as a sticking trombone slide. There's also a little matter of juvenile inadequacy that's equal to putting a square peg in a round hole—ten-year-olds are built with a reach of about twelve inches. Trombone slides are built to require a reach of about twenty-four inches so how the hell is a ten-year-old supposed to make hide nor hair of that…say nothing of music! I hated that thing almost as much as my three older siblings did. They threatened to run over it with the tractor if I didn't stop practicing. That, in fact, became my sole reason to keep going: it was a great way to spite those sons-a-guns!

I was about to run out of steam with the trombone when a darned teacher named Al Gator went and told my mother I was "a natural." I suppose, being a ten-year-old, just a cool name like Al Gator was enough to keep me going for a while but his statement left me with little hope; my mother was suddenly convinced I was to be the next Glenn Miller…she'd never let me quit! The next ten years presented a series of near quitting events.

I've recently been playing with the Swingin' Vermont Big Band, a seventeen-piece big band led by Rich Magnuson whose father, Bob, was one of my first music teachers. Bob plays trombone in that group, and it has been great playing beside a guy who remembers first meeting me as an undersized ten-year-old. He says back then, my right arm was too short to reach sixth and seventh positions so I developed an ingenious way to catch the slide with my big toe. Bob says I didn't do too bad and, even though I never practiced, encouraged me to continue until my arm grew into the job. I'm the lead trombone player in that group and these days Bob, being a drummer-turned-trombone-player, plays beside me. Sometimes I counsel him on his positioning and offer little tidbits of advice. Whenever I make a mistake, though, I always remind him that he "taught me everything I know!"

Arnold Sinclair was another of my early music teachers. He gave private lessons in the basement of Vermont Music Company over in Barre, Vermont. One time I was sitting beside him, laboring through something in the Arbans Method Book. I had to pee, but was too shy to stop the lesson and ask Mr. Sinclair if I could use the bathroom. All of a sudden he stopped the lesson and said, making reference to my swaying knees, "Burr…I don't think you practiced much this week but your rhythm is great." He reached for my trombone, gave me quick directions and I rushed off, not a moment too soon. Arnold Sinclair and I played together much later in life in a brass quintet. One piece in our repertoire was a movement from George Frederic Handel's "Water Music." One time, just as we were about to rehearse the famous piece, Mr. Sinclair burst into laughter and proceeded to tell the story of how I almost peed my pants in the middle of a music lesson…"Water Music!"

Somehow I made it through the end of eighth grade without quitting. All of a sudden I was headed off to Montpelier High School, a daunting thought for a farm kid who had never seen a school with more than one room. The only thing more frightening than MHS to me was the music teacher, Clifton Mix. The stories that I had heard about Mr. Mix left me certain that he picked out less than musically adequate kids, hung them up by their heals until all the talentless blood drained, and then had them for breakfast! I made up my mind to attend one band practice and then quit, thinking that would surely convince my mother that I just wasn't good enough for the big league.

On that feared first day I slinked to the stage of MHS Smiley Auditorium and found a place to open my horn case. The other kids all looked suave and musical to me; some were already seated and making noise that sounded more like burps, farts, and whistles than anything musical. I assembled my horn and found a place at the end of the trombone section, keeping my head bowed and not even acknowledging the kid beside me.

I remember feeling a strange excitement about sitting in a real concert band for the first time. My excitement, however, was fleeting. Suddenly Mr. Mix, a weathered-looking man who walked slightly bow-legged, approached the podium. His gray mustache highlighted what I would learn were trumpet-playing lips; at the moment, though, I viewed them as only dark and sinister. One look at Clifton Mix brought sixty blaring instruments to instant silence.

He quickly laid down the ground rules and started rehearsing the band. Absent my plan, I would have allowed my earlier excitement to grow but instead honed in on all the negatives. When the period, one of the longest hours of my life, finally ended, I packed up my horn for the last time…or so I thought.

Par for my plan, my mother let me off the hook the next day. A couple weeks later, a kid told me that "Old Mix" wanted to see me about something. "What would he want to talk to me for?" I said, dreading the visit already. "I don't know but you'd better do what Mix says," the kid replied.

On the way home that day, I stopped into Mix Music Store and waited just outside the room where he gave private lessons. Inside I heard the faltering sounds of a baritone horn and pitied the poor kid who was blowing it. Finally, the door opened and the red-faced kid came out, carrying a big odd-shaped case. Mr. Mix beckoned me in.

"Why did you quit band?" he asked, twisting those lips up into something better than a frown.

" 'Cause I'm no good," I said hardly audible.

"Why don't you let me decide that? Come back next Tuesday and give it another try...ye don't need to be afraid of me, McGee!" he said in a fake, gruff voice through those now smiling lips (He was an old Navy guy and often substituted "McGee" for our first names).

I did go back the next Tuesday for another try and then every Tuesday for the rest of my high school career. I allowed that strange, good feeling the band gave me to return and I looked forward to band every week. Within three weeks, Mr. Mix upgraded me to first trombone, and I started taking private lessons from him in the room at the back of his store. He was still gruff, but I learned to accept his tirades with a grain of salt. Some of his favorite ones:

"I want more volume, McGee...won't be satisfied till I see lungs come out the bell o' yer horn!"

"If ye don't plan on practicing anymore, McGee, I'm tellin' you to drop that cussed horn in the Winooski on yer way home!"

"Tell yer parents they wasted money on that horn...all it's ever going to make is an expensive lamp!"

"Cross yer legs in my band...I'll chop 'em off at the knees!"

Needless to say, his teaching style would not go over well in this day and age (which is a tragic loss to modern America—his style worked!). For every kid who he chased away, he saved ten, and I was certainly one of the ten. In fact, by my junior year of high school, I took a shine to his daughter Nancy, a fine pianist and euphonium player. Nancy became my first real love, and I spent two years traveling to the Mix Camp over at Lake Champlain and visiting at their Montpelier home. I'll never forget the man who gave me music for a lifetime...well...almost.

In spite of the high school band's offering of social and musical harmony, even with a dash of young love thrown in, it wasn't enough to bridge my next school experience. After I graduated from MHS with mediocre grades, I went to Johnson State College. Back in those days, Johnson's entire Music Department was in an antiquated two-room schoolhouse. Since there wasn't band at Johnson, I put my horn in the closet thinking I would pick it back up at a later date.

My goal at Johnson was to do well enough to transfer after two years to the University of Vermont, a course of action my father had handpicked for me. I wanted, so I thought, to major in plant and soil science at the university which would prepare me to return to the Morse Farm as an expert in growing vegetables. This, I would later find out, was a goal strong enough to suddenly transform me into a straight A student, but was a very weak plan for life. It was my father's plan and not my own. I never developed a passion for plant and soil science, my new school, or the idea of returning to the Morse Farm for life. In the meantime I had lost my interest, lock, stock, and embouchure, in playing the trombone.

On schedule, I transferred to UVM in 1968 as a junior and like the two prior years at Johnson, studied enough to get great grades. At that time I had a Volkswagen Squareback that my brother Elliott had retrofitted with a Beetle engine. Since the taller Beetle engine stuck up into the car, we built a tin box to cover it. The box lacked enough proper insulation to keep the engine noise out and, even worse, the carbon monoxide. I drove that Squareback the thirty-eight miles back to Morse Farm every weekend and school vacation to help my parents with the farm work.

As if the carbon monoxide poisoning and engine noise weren't bad enough for my health, I also managed to drink a lot of beer during that time. My two years at UVM lacked any of the social standing that most of the other students enjoyed. Instead, I got together often with a couple guys to drink beer and verbally bash the out-of-state students. Back then, pot was the substance of choice with most of them. I never got into that much…the two times I tried it, it reminded me of smoking dried horse manure, and it did nothing for my head. My buddies and I wore our beer drinking like badges, though. Looking back at those days, I wonder how we ever survived.

Toward the end of my junior year, the draft lottery had been instated. I ended up with a mid-range draft number, which meant that I had a fifty percent chance of being drafted when I graduated. Since the war in Viet Nam was going hot and heavy in 1969, I was worried about ending up in the middle of it. My friend, Chuck Parker, who had been a tuba player back in the MHS Band, had heard that the Vermont National Guard had a band. I probably would never have looked into it without Chuck's prodding.

We found it headquartered at a modern armory in a suburban part of Burlington. A man named Nick Principe was in charge of Vermont National Guard's 40th Army Band. He met us there one day and reviewed the requirements which included a musical audition, four months of basic and on-the-job training, and then a six-year commitment to the Vermont Army National Guard. It sounded like a viable way to fulfill our commitment and offered a chance to dust off those horns and put them to our lips one more time.

We both passed our auditions and joined. Our basic training was scheduled for the following summer in different places, and although we both came back to play in Vermont's 40th Army Band, our musical paths took different turns. Chuck stayed in ten years and closeted the tuba soon after he left the band. I stayed for fourteen years and grew to love the life of an Army musician. Many of northern Vermont's public school music teachers also played in the band and became my good friends. Through this musical connection and their respect of my abilities as a trombone player, I became a ringer for civilian musical groups from jazz combos to community musicals. I haven't put that trombone down since…what Clifton Mix started, the U.S. Army rekindled.

Sometimes I wonder why music has been so huge in my life, as seven-day-a-week farming was the living I chose long ago. Playing gigs till all hours at night and winding my way back to Morse Farm at 2 a.m. seems counter to farming; sorry, but I just had to do it! But my tales of music can't end quite yet even though I'm sure that I have made my point. I must take care of the matter of musical legacy.

My sons, Robby and Tommy, grew up aware of my musical drive. They saw me head out carrying that trombone night after night and when it was possible, went with me. I've always credited my wife, Betsy, with giving the boys their music because she's the one who made them practice. That old adage, however, about leaves not falling far from trees also kicked in… quite appropriate, I suppose, for a family of maple tree farmers.

Rob is a trombone-turned-bass player and Tom is a trumpet player. They both have musical wings far broader and more advanced than my own, and I could not be more proud. Rob now attends City College of New York as a music performance major and Tom works at Morse Farm by day and plays trumpet by night.

People often ask if the boys and I play music together and my answer, in all honesty, is "not enough." The fact that they play together, however, is enough to sustain me forever. The two Morse boys grew up close in age with a common love of music. They often appear in the same group; Betsy and I will go, sit in the audience, and gloat over the Morse boys' skill and sensitivity as Vermont musicians.

Speaking of Betsy, the marriage that I gave only a few months is now half way through its thirtieth year. Our anniversary is March 19 and our boys honored us last year with a gift certificate for a night at the Mount Washington Hotel. We recently went over there and had a wonderful time. Our room overlooked the long road that leads to the hotel from busy Route 302. From that perspective, Mount Washington Hotel appears regal and majestic; I thought of my own road that started behind that Glenwood stove. It's long and has led through many traffic jams and pileups, but from my present perch, offers views of things regal and majestic. Thanks to my Vermont heritage, I continue to enjoy the sweetness of the world's best maple syrup, the harshness of a cold winter, and the contrast of being able to say "to hell with it all" and go off to play music.

Burr Morse

Introduction

BY ROBINSON MORSE

This much I can say with certainty, there are few better ways to grow up than on a farm in Vermont, sugaring, raising crops, and just enjoying the outdoors. As far as preparation for the world at large and all of the challenges one faces negotiating it, my own background has given me everything I need and then some. As I have traveled and met people and encountered situations of every stripe, I am more and more aware of how fortunate I am to have been raised the way I was by the family that surrounds me to this day.

If you are reading this right now, chances are you already know quite a bit about my family and its long tradition of making syrup and scratching out a living in Vermont. Either because you have read my father's first book, *Sweet Days & Beyond*, or because you have visited the farm and taken in the sights, smells, and sounds of sugaring, you know the setting and a little about the mentality that drives us Vermont sugarmakers. It is this mentality, this set of personality traits and their accompanying outlook, that I am most thankful for.

The outlook that I speak of varies somewhat from sugarmaker to sugarmaker but always has a balance of two main components, healthy optimism and what I'd like to call realistic pessimism. The remaining ingredients amount to a blend of strong work ethic and the patience and will to succeed, even if it kills you. It is these qualities that my ancestors and immediate family have instilled in me and it seems to me they are less and less common in today's world. Knowing that things will eventually work out but that there are bound to be hitches and glitches along the way is just plain common sense. And to have the stubborn drive to get to the bottom of these daily problems is important but not to be taken for granted. Now if even a few of our policymakers and public figures shared genetic traits with my forefathers, we would be in better shape as a nation for certain.

When I look ahead at my life and the path in front of me, I honestly cannot predict where I will end up or how things will pan out. The world is changing for us all and the ways and means of the past are transforming in front of our eyes. Even the weather and the climate are behaving differently and more extremely. In this way, life for all people might start to more closely resemble Vermont living where, "if you don't like the weather, just wait five minutes!"

Wherever it all leads, I am so glad to have the solid and Vermont-sweetened genes that I do.

Part One

Growin' Up

Chapter 1

A Safe Passage

MY DEAR MOTHER, DOT MORSE, passed into the great beyond last Sunday. We'd sat with her for days knowing she was going away, at least the part of her that we could be with and hold. But we knew the other part of her, the part even bigger than life — the light that shone through her, would be with us forever. So let's make a deal—I'll write and while you read, let that light shine. Her light will keep us all happy.

I was the youngest of the litter and my nickname kind of got thrown at me. They say my sister Susie, who was three, couldn't quite handle "Baby Brother" and shortened it to "Burr." Somehow that name grabbed hold of my attitude too! I felt vulnerable, likely to be picked off at any moment like a burr under a saddle. For a long while my mother was my haven, my world, my shining light. In my first two years I often snuggled into the folds of her long dress and clung close to her warmth. The few times I strayed, it was behind our old Glenwood kitchen stove, another warm place and always in sight of mama.

Memories of her warmth and protection have followed me throughout my life. One, in particular, is of a trip to the neighbors in our '51 Mercury. Susie and I sat on the front seat, close to our mother, peering at the expanse of buttons and dimples on the dashboard. Our mother drove that huge old boat-of-a car. She sat straight, both hands on the steering wheel, straining to see beyond the long hood to the road ahead. We sat, pasted to the back of the seat like little Raggedy Anns and Andys, knowing the road led to the house of two old maids, Gerty and Glee. Their farmhouse was on the other side of the hill from our place and we went there often. They had a grandfather clock that tocked and ticked, pleasantly conflicting with the spring-fed drip somewhere in their kitchen. They used words like "gracious," and "mercy sakes," and always had a full candy jar on their round oak table. We loved them for their candy but called them "Dirty and Pee" behind their backs— typical brats, we were.

The gravel road to their place went through a glen, to us dark and scary. Cox Turn stood midway in the glen on the brow of a hill. My mother was a slow, careful driver and every time she approached Cox Turn she honked the horn to warn other motorists that we were there. She slowed to a creep but before she started her wide left-hand sweep, she positioned her right arm straight out in front of us. Back in those days, before seat belts and child seats, we felt safety through trust and the strength of our mother's protective arm.

I began testing and stretching the umbilical cord after a fashion. One time, after we moved to our new farm, I went exploring the brook that flowed through our property and down into the Winooski River. I moved like a dog with its nose to the ground, each stream-bank stone led to another and before long, I had gone through a deep wood and crossed under several highways. Just before I reached the confluence with the Winooski, a scream woke me from my stupor. I looked around and there was an extremely agitated Dot Morse, still dressed in her apron. She had tracked me all that distance, led by "mother's instinct" and worry. She hustled me up a steep bank to the road where our '55 Plymouth stood. She plunked me on the back seat to fend for myself that time, and drove home faster than usual.

She was always doing little things to protect us. She brought four of us up to adulthood and on toward old age while teaching school and being an equal partner with our dad on the farm. She could do anything. The other night, when we were with her and knew she was slipping away, oh how I wish I could have honked my horn and put my arm out to keep her from going, but that happy light led her away. I assume it was as natural as following a brook, one stream-bank stone at a time, to a place where our father, Harry, patiently waited. One neighbor recently said, "Dot's going to be a splendid angel." Those two words, "splendid angel," brought tears to my eyes. They were happy tears and I knew my mother had simply added to her résumé: loving housewife, mother, teacher, protector and splendid angel. She'll be watching from there.

Chapter 2

The Blink of An Eye

I'VE ALWAYS HAD annoying facial tics that come alive with lots of eye blinking, cheek scrunching and impulsive nods of my head. In my sixty years of living with them, I've developed the skills of camouflage, postponement, or avoidance; in other words, I often turn my head to blink, count to ten before I scrunch, and never, ever go to auctions! Betsy constantly reminds me of my incessant throat clearing but, being the angel that she is, has put up with me for some thirty-one years now. Although I have never had an official diagnosis, I'm sure that I have at least a mild form of the condition called Tourette's Syndrome. When I looked up the definition, I was more certain than ever: "Simple vocal tics may include throat-clearing, sniffing/snorting, grunting, or barking. More complex vocal tics include words or phrases." I've never barked or inappropriately sworn (when I swear, I always mean it!) but I once did involuntarily belch into my trombone while playing at a funeral. It was at a point where the music was pianissimo but the belch came out the bell fortissimo and foul...not good!

I would never want to make fun of folks with special problems but, being one of them, I also am aware that "life goes on" and we might just as well make the best of it. There are some funny stories out there about these personal bloopers.

My father told me a story once about an old man named Charlie whose barks and snorts were always accompanied by tobacco chewing. One day after church, Dad recalled that folks were lined up exchanging pleasantries with the preacher just outside on the church steps. Dad was just a boy and he and his buddy, Kenneth Fowler, had deviltry on their minds as boys will after sitting through a long church service. They knew that Charlie had a huge wad of tobacco in his mouth. They also knew that cues from the outside sometimes triggered his idiosyncrasies. Kenneth began sneaking through the shrubbery until he was just behind Charlie who stood directly in front of the preacher at point blank range. Suddenly, like a Roman warrior, young Kenneth shouted "spit quick!" Dad said that preacher ended up with slimy, brown goop from his white pate down to his starched clerical collar...a surprise ending to a long service!

Sometimes these sudden bursts of personality come via the character factor rather than any neurological disorder. Stubby Martin was a character. He grew up around Maple Corner and, from an early age, put his Type A personality to work developing little spurts of wit and one-liners. He never took a shine to school but acquired great skills as a Yankee trader as he grew up. Stubby eventually became one of the region's most popular auctioneers, a vocation that allowed him to use both his witty one-liners and his skill as a Yankee trader. I recently heard a story about Stubby after old age had stepped in to exaggerate his already colorful outbursts.

Stubby and his wife, Ethelyn, had attended the funeral of one of his stepbrothers. It was a long, drawn-out affair where, in addition to the usual rituals, folks were invited to offer remarks about the deceased. Ethelyn said when it started into hour three, she began to worry about her husband's ability to sit and be quiet, but Stubby behaved very well right through the final, solemn prayer. It was at the "Amen," however, when Stubby Martin had finally had enough. Suddenly he clapped his hands together, rose to a standing position and hollered "BINGO" at the top of his lungs!

I recently asked Ethelyn if the story was true and if she'd mind if I wrote about it. She said it was indeed true. "I was so embarrassed," she laughed."Stub went up and I went down!" Ethelyn said Stubby, who recently passed away, would have been pleased that I thought of him and that I was welcome to write it up. I knew him well enough to know she was right...for the world to be entertained a little at his expense would have seemed a great bargain to Stubby Martin and he'd ought to know...he was a Yankee trader.

The more news I hear these days, the more I think anything that's light and humorous is a great bargain. There's too much doom and gloom out there so let's all concentrate on more laughter. Sure, today's humor came largely at the expense of church and folks with tics but that's OK...I know God takes a Stubby Martin attitude toward good clean fun and we might as well enjoy ourselves because life can change with the blink of an eye.

Chapter 3

Come Boss, Go Boss

SINCE MID-SUMMER is a cow's time of year with all the luscious green-grass around, my mind is in bovine gear these days. Here are a couple of thoughts on the subject of cows crossing the road...moooove over chickens!

A while back I had a music gig down at the Woodstock Inn in Woodstock, Vermont. A beautiful summer evening accompanied me from Bethel down past the upscale properties of Barnard and into the valley that leads to Woodstock. Being a native Vermonter, I've always looked a little askance at Woodstock because of its Rockefeller influence and moneyed image. The other night, however, I realized that no amount of money or social status can take Vermont out of Woodstock, or, for that matter, cows!

I was traveling along at 50 mph, enjoying the country air through wide-open windows (no air conditioning for this Vermonter) when the road rounded one of the valley's dumpling-like hills. All of a sudden, 1960s nostalgia came whooshing in with the fresh, country air; there in front of my car was a herd of cattle being driven across the road to night pasture.

I stopped 200 feet away and put my car in park...cows own the road, you know. The herd, mostly Jerseys peppered lightly with Holsteins, stepped out of a red barn and followed a manure-dabbed swath across the black-top. Two young men with canes stood by tiredly, tapping an occasional rump and no doubt muttering an occasional "get along now." They reminded me of myself forty plus years ago.

We used to cross cows just like that and motorists used to stop in honor of the rule. Those few who didn't were either met by a quick, dent-causing whap on their hood by our canes, or worse, had their number reported to the police, who understood that "cows own the road." Then it all went away...dairy farmers sold out in droves and the huge farms that were left began keeping their cows under a roof, 24/7. I miss those days, yes I do, and the other night was not only a gentle burst of nostalgia but ten whole milk minutes in today's boring 1% world. I later learned that the cows belonged to the Lewis family and the event is locally known as "The Crossing of the Girls." It's too bad that cow crossings are so rare these days that cute names have to be attached to them; nevertheless, I'm thankful for one family that still wants to do it the good old way and, by the way, kudos Woodstock, Vermont.

I'll start my next cow-crossing tale with the words on a sign that M. Walter Smith used to have over at his Plainfield, Vermont, place: "Slow down... we pasture this road!" That was the attitude, written or unwritten, until the litigious society came along and minimized cows' rights—reminds me of a story my friend Warner Shedd told me recently about my father.

Warner, our new Washington County forester, and his wife, Edie, had just moved into a house down the road from our barn. It was the early 1960s and he, being a budding bureaucrat, knew all about the changing world. He and Edie came home late one night and noticed a single cow grazing on the wrong side of the road from the rest of my father's herd. Warner, concerned that the beast might cause an accident, drove over to our house and knocked at the door. He thought it was serious enough to wake my father up even though they weren't acquainted much yet. Warner said my father was a long time responding but finally appeared in his bathrobe and sleepily opened the door.

"Yes," Dad said.

"Mr. Morse...I'm sorry to bother you," Warner said, "but you have a cow out down the road...thought you'd ought to know."

(Long pause) "Oh?" my father said.

"Yup...could be a problem," Warner persisted, sensing that my father was beginning to question the need for the interruption of his sleep.

(Long pause) "Just one?" my father questioned again.

"Yup," a blushing Warner replied.

At that, Harry Morse closed both the conversation and the door with the words, "I'll have t'think about that."

When Warner told me the story, my first thought was that Harry Morse, much out of keeping for Harry Morse, was being a bit rude. Warner, however, remembers the incident with his humor intact. He grew up on a dairy farm down in Ferrisburgh, Vermont, and therefore knew something about the menacing nature of bovines. He also knew that 5 a.m. milking comes pretty darned early for farmers like Harry Morse and a midnight wakeup is hardly ever appropriate. I'm sure he debated just leaving well enough alone but ended up erring on the side of "changing times," times when cows would no longer own the road.

Keep your fences mended.

Chapter 4

Boys'll Be Boys

A LOT OF KIDS have been coming in the sugarhouse lately. Kids come in all shapes, sizes and, like salsa, different levels of "zing." I like my salsa mild and appreciate the same in my sugarhouse visitors, given all of the hot, sticky ways kids can get in trouble in that place. The other day my old friend Jeff Bean came in. I was complaining about a recent group of kids who were loosely chaperoned and medium plus on the salsa scale. He chuckled and reminded me of a time when I, yes "little old Burr," was somewhere between Mexican jumping bean and red hot jalapeno.

Jeff and I grew up together. We lived less than a mile from each other, fished the local brooks, skated the frozen ponds, and built humongous ski jumps on a steep hill across from his house. When it was my turn to entertain, however, I usually led the way to a special world of caverns, mazes, slides and dead falls, a place where we could run miles, make fantastic discoveries, expend haymow-sized energy, and never run out of hiding places without ever going outside. That place was our dairy farm which, in those days, started at the new barn and went on through alleyways, old barns, horse barns, and carriage rooms, all the way to my grandparents' comfortable home. Folks often ask me why old New England farms were built that way and my best explanation is: "It's more fun for kids, of course!"

I remember the bedding bin, which started on the ground level in the old barn and rose up into a mountain of pine-sweet sawdust. We'd climb up on timbers close to the barn's peak and dare each other to jump. The twenty-five-foot jump was scary as all get out but very character building. The downy-soft landing brought giggles of delight and repeated trips to even higher places. Beyond the bedding bin, a hundred tons of hay bales went on forever, and we spent hours rearranging them into forts and mountain passes. Then there were the dark recesses where those of us brazen enough would go with the ghosts and the barn cats, and then come back heroes. Close to the dark recesses lived Sparky, the bull. Bulls, rest all their souls, have been replaced these days by breeding technicians with frozen semen and long utensils. Back when I was a boy, however, Sparky was an integral farm employee whose out-of-the-way abode drew minimal visits except for boys with red hot jalapeno designs.

Sparky, when left to his own devices, was glad to while the "off" hours chewing his cud and burping sour hay residue. To us boys, however, old Spark provided strange levels of education, adventure, and intrigue. One time, several of us approached him from different flanks, commandos in the dark. It was a well organized campaign, complete with flashlight signals and contingency plans, sans one — my grandparents. Jeff said the sling-shots were my idea. At first Sparky just got a little huffy, but my well- placed whap to his "manhood" with a marble-sized pebble really set him off. His rude snorts turned to an extended bawl and then he began to paw the bottom of his stall. All of a sudden he lunged at the plank sides, like a wreaking ball gone berserk. Jeff recalls hearing me say "We better get out of here before they come down." He said I stressed the word "they" and swiveled my eyes toward the stairs that led to the farmhouse. We pictured dishes falling from cupboards and a wise grandpa heading to the bullpen, switch in hand. Jeff said we evaporated into the haymow, like rats in the light, and frittered away plenty of time before we showed our faces again.

My grandparents never directly mentioned the "bull episode" but I'm sure they felt the tremors in their house. They were wise folks that way, wise enough to realize a childhood prank or two could be met with turned heads. I'll never forget those old buildings and the good times they provided for our group of hell-raisers, though most of the structures disappeared while I was a teenager. My grandfather, the businessman, saw too many roofs to roof and sills to repair for a farm economy that was changing. About the time old Sparky and his kind got replaced by breeding technicians, grandpa tore the whole thing down. My boys now live in the farmhouse, which stands a short distance from the solitary "new barn." Sometimes when I'm over there, I look at the void between the two and visualize how it used to be. I see ghosts of the old complex and wish my boys could have seen it and, better yet, had the run of it.

I've spent most of my life since those times in a "sweet" business, maybe to make amends for the hellion I was. I don't regret it for a minute, though, no-sireee. One thing I know for sure is, whether it's in a steamy sugarhouse, jumping in the sawdust, or taunting an innocent animal, boys will always be boys.

Chapter 5

The Politics of Bulldozers

I SUPPOSE the old codgers would say this winter doesn't deserve braggin' rights but, wait just a gol-derned minute, I'm close enough to an old codger now so that I can brag about anything I want and I'd compare this winter to the best, uhh worst of 'em. It did start out like a weak cup-a-coffee but it sure as hell ended up espresso on Valentine's Day!

Valentine's Day brought a whole winter's worth of snow in eight hours, leavin' us all scrambling to clean up and the guys with four-wheel-drive plow trucks droppin' like fleas; reminds me of a storm once back in the '60s when we had to call in the heavy artillery.

That time snow fell so fast that barns were falling down, folks were stranded in their homes, and those plow trucks were as worthless as broken shovels. The only thing that would handle that snow was Aunt Betsy, our big old bulldozer. Aunt Betsy was getting quite tired at that time. Her tracks were about worn out and would fall off at the very hint of a side hill, but she would push like a rushing army on a straightaway. Normally, blacktop roads are off limits for bulldozers but due to the situation, Aunt Betsy and I headed up the County Road to open up driveways.

Folks were really appreciative to see us coming. They all offered to pay me, but I refused — said maybe I'd be stranded sometime and need a hand. When I got to the Tracy Farm, however, Amelia Tracy watched from her kitchen door as I pushed mountains of snow this way and that way. When I finished, she beckoned me in and I knew there was no refusin' Amelia Tracy. I entered an anteroom where barn frocks and coveralls hung at the ready, covering one whole wall. Amelia protested from close by, "Don't bother to take your boots off —it's only water." I stepped up to a bootjack and pulled 'em off anyway, knowing it was the right thing to do. My nose led me into a high-ceilinged kitchen where she stood frying donuts at an ancient cook stove. "Sit right down Burr, I've just taken that platter full out of the fat." I sat at the kitchen table in front of the platter and gorged myself on those heavenly donuts, totally unbothered by the word "fat."

I'm reminded of another story about a tired old bulldozer: There was once a Vermont town that had an article on the Town Meetin' agenda about buying a new bulldozer. Before debate got started, a man asked if the road commissioner could come forward and answer some questions. The commissioner ambled to the front of the hall, a tired-looking man hardly used to public speaking.

"What d'you wanta know about the bulldozer?" he asked.

"Well, sir," the man asked, "that bulldozer looks OK to me. Can't we keep using it?"

The commissioner cradled his grizzled chin with his right hand, furrowed his forehead and replied, "Welllll...I don't know...that we couldn't get by...for a few more years...the only problem with th'old one is that it'll only turn left."

I never heard how the vote came out but I'm sure the hall erupted in laughter over the left-turnin' bulldozer! I can also imagine some mighty creative mud-slingin'; the liberals might accuse the conservatives of clinging to a left-turning bulldozer even if it has to go clear round the world to get back to square one. On the other hand, the conservatives might charge the libs with buying a whole fleet of new ones...that would still only turn left!

I happen to know the story is not that far fetched, 'cause after Aunt Betsy and Amelia Tracy passed on, I ended up with one a them left-turnin' bulldozers myself. It was a John Deere 10-10, a real dawg of a machine. It wouldn't of pushed its way out of a wet paper bag but, by golly, if I could have gotten another of Amelia Tracy's donuts, I'd have driven it clear round the world.

Chapter 6

Camping Farmer Style

IT'S THE TIME of year when folks are thinking of getting out into the wide open countryside, taking in the fresh air and giving their cares a grand shove off. It's vacation time and I'm thinking of the most nostalgia-packed of vacations—camping. Being in the tourism business, I meet a lot of camping people and am always amazed at the diversity among them. Take, for instance, my friend Erv Steinmann who showed up last sugar season with enough stuff to sink a canoe, all packed in a tiny Toyota RAV-4. It looked, frankly, like a war zone inside there, but Erv swore he found a place to curl up and sleep. There's all shapes and sizes of campers, from the humble Corolla-towed pop-up to the converted tour bus that takes half of Yellowstone to turn around. Yup, modern Americana is full of camping opportunities but they can't hold a candle to my camping experience long ago when camp fires were real and mosquitoes were BIG.

Back then, before interstate highways and modern-day theme parks, camping involved tons of creativity. Folks stayed closer to home and either simply pitched a tent or crammed into a funny little humped-backed trailer. We were dairy farmers and it was hard to get away, what with the seven-day-a-week barn chores and haying. There were a few years, however, when we had a good hired man and managed to vacation at a magical place up on Lake Champlain in Alburg, Vermont. It had two beautiful sand beaches, cedar-clad bluffs and the best part of all, built-in privacy; you see, it was owned by two elderly brothers whose interest was in milking Holsteins rather than developing what was to become the most desirable piece of land this side of Niagara Falls. They liked us because we were farmers, so the place was ours for a gallon of syrup and a pledge to keep our mouths shut.

Being farmers, we made do with what we had; our spirit of adventure more than made up for our lack of camping know-how. A big Chevrolet farm truck served as our camper. Dad, the king of Yankee ingenuity, cut maple saplings and fashioned hoops above its platform bed. Over the hoops, he stretched a huge canvas. We furnished it with mattresses from our own beds and enough paraphernalia to service a small army. It was a proud day when we headed out with that rig, somewhere between late covered wagon and early motor home in the evolution of campers.

Approaching the Palmer Brothers' farm was like going back in time with a view. Against a cheerful backdrop of Lake Champlain, dilapidated farm buildings stood surrounded by the last gasps of board fences. We crept into the yard with the big Chevy and stopped by two cars, one pulling a funny-looking trailer fashioned with airplane parts. Those cars were spilling with aunts, uncles and cousins; you see, our "farmer immunity" extended to a few special relatives. For a kid like me, the only thing that could improve a week in paradise was to have cousins to play with.

As we pulled up, the two tired-looking Palmer brothers approached my father —farmer, diplomat. We kept our excitement at bay until their hand-shake was complete and then headed toward an electric fence gate that my older brother held open. Our favorite campsite stood in the distance, beyond a sand beach cove that the pasture road curved around. Our cara-van ground around the cove and up the last hill. We stopped at a clearing on top of a huge bluff where two clumps of cedars framed a grand view of the Adirondacks. The first thing we did was to pull an 18-foot extension ladder from the Chevy's long bed. It would be our stairway to the water's jagged edge and two nearby beaches.

We have no tales of the quintessential pesky camp bears or raccoons but we sure had cows! We shared the site with the Palmers' herd of Holsteins. Besides supplying us with plenty of dried cow chips for Frisbee throwing, they also left fresh ones, once even right plumb in the middle of my moth-er's cooking pot! Although it was tempting to angrily drive them away, we honored them as landlords; we were the tenants. One time we came back from an afternoon of swimming to find remnants of two bushels of sweet corn, our garden's entire offering, scattered and mauled: the Holsteins stood close by with satisfied looks on their faces.

Camping at Alburg was a fleeting thing in the scheme of things but a day there was better than a trip around the world to us. A few nights ago my cousin David, a camera buff, dropped off a picture of my parents in the back of that old Chevy truck. My parents, both gone now, looked like Ma and Pa Kettle and probably smelled like 'em, too! The picture showed them dealing with some kind of camping emergency, like possibly throwing a large garter snake out of a sleeping bag, but their faces were youthful and sported huge grins; they were having a ball! Some folks these days think that a bigger motor home or a longer trip translates to more fun, but I know better. Yes sir, even though I haven't been camping for fifty years, I've gained some wisdom along the way: like Mother Nature, you don't fool with nostalgia. One week with those cows, that old truck, and a big, loving family —now that's as good as it gets!

Chapter 7
Dealin' Friendship

THE OTHER MORNING as I headed out our lower drive for a meeting over in Norwich, my son's two yearling Herefords stood grazing in the pasture to the left...pretty as a picture, they were. My dad and I used to run sixty of those same red and white critters in that pasture but sold out twenty-five years ago to a guy who said he'd pay us in a few weeks...Dad's passed on and I'm still waitin' for the check. I'm proud that Tommy wants to get back into it and trust that he'll be a little more business savvy than we were. Before I got on I-89 heading east, I stopped in Montpelier for gas... Yaaaouch...$3.65 a gallon and climbing! For some reason, thoughts of the pastoral scene I had just left melded with the idea of getting "skinned" and I began thinking about cattle dealers.

Being a farmer, I was born with a low-grade distrust of cattle dealers. I've tried to shake it over the years but it still follows me at the ripe age of sixty. I thought of a sale barn over in Corinth which Dad and I used to visit when I was a kid. It was run by the Gallerani family, a clan as steeped in cattle dealing as we were in dairy farming. They closed down the sale barn years ago and started up the Farm Way store in Bradford. I had never been to Farm Way and an early ending meeting helped me make up my mind; I would follow a different "cow path" home and drive the short distance to Bradford to see what old cattle dealers look like.

I found the Farm Way store on VT Route 25, just a hop and a skip from the Connecticut River. It was clear from the odd mixture of fence posts, stock watering tubs, kayaks and Adirondack chairs outside, that marketing around this place included a higher understanding of demographics. When I entered and asked to see Mrs. Gallerani, the usual screening about who I was and what I wanted was pleasantly absent..."I'll page Bobbi," the cashier said.

I waited at the business end of a place that appeared to ramble into barn-sized spaces and multi-levels. In less than five minutes, a pretty, grey-haired woman dressed for Madison Avenue approached. Bobbi Gallerani and I shook hands and when she heard my name, it was like we had known each other forever. As we talked, a short, husky man emerged from the back room. Paul, her husband, would prove to be one of the friendliest folks I've ever met. He remembered my grandpa, Sydney, and seemed pleased that I would pay him a visit. Soon, I was following him on a tour of the store. Paul walked at a hurried clip, oddly projecting that he had both a huge amount to do and a world of time for me. We stopped often while he pointed out special parts of the store or answered the walkie-talkie that he palmed at the ready.

It seemed like we had walked through acres under roofs when we reached a section where they sold furniture. We each chose a plush chair to flop on and began talking about the old days of cattle sales and the complications of running a business today. Several times he used the expression "I'm almost seventy-one, you know," somehow failing to convince me that this man was capable of slowing down. As we talked, Bobbi appeared and sat in a sofa opposite us. I asked Paul if he had any tales of cattle dealin' that I might write about. He hesitated, used those words, "I'm almost seventy-one" one more time and then merged into a well-remembered tale of returning from the commission sale up in Swanton one time.

"I was just a kid," he said. "Dad sent me up to Swanton to buy a load of cattle with a truck that only hauled ten. I shoulda' known better, but I bought eleven and crowded 'em all in. I was headin' home in the middle of the night and got to Williston when I checked on the cows...two of 'em were down and I knew I had to do something. I drove till I saw a barnyard with a gate, backed up to the gate and turned 'em loose." He said when he went back the next morning to claim his cows the farmer was kind of surprised to see the extra cows in his yard but didn't say much. "He helped me load 'em back in and I thanked him for the use of his yard." In today's Williston, home to Wal-Mart, Home Depot and Circuit City, an episode like that would surely involve the entire police department, several lawyers and the SPCA!

Another time, Paul said he paid for a herd of pregnant cows but when he got them home and had them checked, they were all barren...the farmer he bought them from had lied about the presence of a bull. I was not surprised when he said many of his deals over the years had gone sour but just before we headed toward the parking lot, he turned to me and said with a broad grin and a wink of his eye, "We made some money, too, you know."

I had no trouble believing that, thinking of the sprawling store which offered everything plus the kitchen sink, but I'm the one who drove away that day feeling rich...richly blessed with some new friends and a change of heart about farmers and cattle dealers.

Chapter 8

The Crawford Lot

OVER ON THE EASTERN side of our farm is a piece of land we call the Crawford Lot. When I was a boy I loved to go over there exploring. The Crawford Lot offered a magnificent view of Camel's Hump to the west. On just the right summer days, there'd be wild strawberries by the luscious millions growing around the ledge outcroppings. Another thing that loved the ledges were huge, spreading juniper bushes which usually stood guard over discarded farm and household things; often, with a little digging, I'd find a big, ancient dump...heaven to a boy like me! Sometimes my father and I would go there with the old bulldozer trying, usually in vain, to coax the land around these places into usable farmland. Once he pointed to some rounded parallel contours. "Potatahs," he said. "That's where old Crawford musta grown his potatahs." My father helped me visualize the evolution of land and the different folks who worked it through the ages.

Crawford was one of those folks, a farmer long ago, back when land was measured in usable places between the ledges. After he was gone, we used to put dry cows and young stock over there on the Crawford Lot, then the trees started to grow up. Land's fickle, like people; some of it took to white pines, some to spruce and fir, but each part of the Crawford Lot blossomed with its own whiskery personality. At first we cursed the eyesore and went there with chain saws trying to beat the place back into pasture, but that never works with nature in charge. The trees grew, looking a little neater every year. Soon we had a little forest instead of open pasture and I began to dream of shadowy places beneath the growing timber.

I love to log. I'm never happier than when I'm in the woods with a chain saw. "Trees need room to grow," said the forester. "You'll have a great harvest here one day if you thin 'em out in a sensible way." That sounded good to me, so I went in and thinned, visualizing a day when the pines were as big around as storage drums and the spruce and fir stood tall and strong. The forester urged me to get some help and recommended horse loggers…"easier on the land…leave fewer damaged trees," he said.

The horse loggers appeared one winter day in a beat-up Dodge pickup with a weathered plank bed. Following the pickup was a cattle truck which had been hired to haul two huge Belgian work horses. The loggers' names were Theron and Theron; quite possibly father and son but my speculation was obscured by their floppy winter hats, and faces sporting week-old stubble and thick layers of axle grease. Theron and Theron had previously built makeshift paddocks on the property in a grove of thick, young firs. A pile of baled hay stood nearby under a tarp and the makeshift paddocks had been installed with comfort in mind; even though the two loggers showed outward signs of being a little "slow," they obviously loved their horses.

Every day I heard chain saws buzzing over there in the Crawford Lot and one day I decided to go check on their progress. I grabbed my seasoned Sachs Dolmar chain saw and headed out; I'm never comfortable in the woods without a chain saw. As I approached the thickest part of the forest, I heard a buzzing and the crash of a falling tree. Strangely there was a second buzzing nearby in the other direction. "Why wouldn't they work as a team?" I thought heading toward the second logger. As I got close, the buzzing had turned into a ratcheting *drdrdrdrdrdrrr…drdrdrdrdrrr …drdrdrdrdrdrrr* and human swearing, sounds that always accompany a chain saw that will not start. Suddenly there was a *whoosh* before my eyes and a *crash* to my left. I looked over to see a vintage chain saw tumble from its point of impact down to the base of a large spruce tree. A glance to my right presented the logger who sat, head in hands, muttering "Gaw nam fing…I hate dat fumbitch!"

I walked over to him and placed the Sachs Dolmar at his feet. "Here," I said. "Use this until yours gets fixed." He looked up with friendly eyes. "Fanks," he said. His horse stood a distance away, waiting patiently, and I asked him why the two loggers didn't work together with one horse… made more sense to me than one person having to fell trees, buck logs, and handle a skid horse all at once.

"But we got two husses," he said. "Besides that, you work wi' Feron a while, Feron fink he own you!"

" 'Nough said," I responded. "I kinda like to work alone in the woods myself."

These days our cross-country ski trails sweep through the Crawford Lot. The other day I skied there and stopped at a spot that once offered wild strawberries by the luscious millions and stunning views to the west. Now, I stood in the dark shadows under pine trees as big around as storage drums. The expression, "Well done, old friend" kept coming to mind. I smiled and skied away, wondering what kind of show the Crawford Lot would put on for the next generation.

Chapter 9

Fair Merchandizing

IT'S THAT TIME of year here in Vermont when the fairs, like the leaves, come out in full color. Because I make part of my living from the colored leaves, I don't normally have much time to attend fairs. When I do, however, I go to the Tunbridge World's Fair, the rootin'-tootin'est gol dang fair east of Iowa. Last year Claude Stone, the tech guy at Morse Farm, and I drove down to Tunbridge one evening, just a pleasant drive through Vermont hill country. The village of Tunbridge nestles among wicked steep hillsides of mixed pastures and maple groves. The fairgrounds lie at the bottom, as if spilled from the hillsides. They stretch along a pristine river's flood plain, where a few flat hay fields mix with lumpy terrain left over from the spilling —geographically speaking it's a hell of a place for a fair.

The word "World" was added to Tunbridge Fair's nomenclature some years ago because of its worldwide reputation, a reputation that has grown faster than a 300- pound zucchini. These days Tunbridge is tame enough for family fun but it used to be "so wild and wooly that 'sober' individuals were turned out as 'nuisances,'" as related in Virtual Vermont Internet Magazine. Stories of the brawlin' at Tunbridge Fair are so rampant that a visit there is always a bit of a tongue-in-cheek experience. Last year when Claude and I went, we parked in a field overflowing with automobiles and entered the fairgrounds over a plank bridge that spans the river. The distinct smell of fresh hay and cow manure greeted us midway across the bridge, a proper welcome, I'd say, to the rootin'-tootin'est of fairs. The crowd immediately swept us into a ceremonial walk through the cow barns, horticultural displays, and midway—ceremonial, I say, because we were not interested in any of that stuff, we just went for the food! We proceeded to eat enough grease to fill up a fun house before we finally waddled away, satisfied with our Fair experience 2005.

Speaking of food (and confessions, since my dear wife, Betsy, thinks I ate my last Italian sausage sometime in the late 70s), I remember one time when I was a young man, working at the Tunbridge Fair and, yes, partaking of the spirits. Our most addictively delicious sweet corn, Silver Queen, was so bountiful that year that we had to get creative with marketing. Dad came up with the idea of selling corn-on-the-cob at the Tunbridge Fair and asked fellow maple sugarmaker Shorty Danforth if we could share space in his snack bar. They agreed on a fair rent and then Dad appointed me in charge of the project. The first day, after getting up at 4 a.m. to do all my picking, I pulled into the fairgrounds a few minutes before opening and met Shorty's son, Bill, who would be my landlord for the next four days. I offered to pay my rent in advance but Bill waved me back with typical Vermont righteousness: "We're both sugarmakers. We just shook hands. That's trust enough for me."

I got a chance that first day to test the market and hone my primitive skills as a carnival barker/short order cook. Sales, however, were flat and I went home that night wondering if our venture was going to work. The next day, after a sleepless night filled with Yankee scheming, I arrived at Tunbridge armed with a pickup load of fresh Silver Queen and a secret ingredient. I peeled some corn and lit the burners under the maple sugar pan I was using, pouring a goodly amount of Grade B maple syrup into the corn water. By mid morning I had a huge lines of customers at the Danforth Snack Bar drawn by the best darned sweet corn in the world, and the heavenly fragrance of boiling maple water!

In fact, by mid afternoon I had sold all my corn. Being giddy with my newfound success, I stuffed the proceeds into my pockets and headed out around the fairgrounds only to end up back at the bluff beside Danforth's hamburger stand with a stash of beer. I sat drinking beer and was soon joined by a woman, not at all uncommon for Tunbridge of those days. As the day wore on we got louder and louder and one thing led to another. All of a sudden I felt Bill Danforth's hand on my shoulder. "Uh...Burr," he said, "come to think of it, I'll take that rent now." Bill, seasoned at Tunbridge Fair psychology, had seen the handwriting on the wall — many a farm boy had gone astray with a pocketful of money and a strange woman at the Tunbridge Fair!

I never did go back to work at the fair after that year but it was a good way to sell my surplus Silver Queen and it taught me a thing or two about merchandising to boot. Bill Danforth and I have been great friends ever since. Every once in a while I kid him about not trusting me. "Hell," he always says, "you're honest enough but you never know what's going to happen at the Tunbridge Fair!" In a way he's wrong — I know I'll go back this year for my fix of quintessential Vermont and some greasy fair food.

Chapter 10

A Fall into Grace

I'VE BEEN OUT in the sugarbush the last few days tinkering on the tubing lines in the frigid cold. We're about to enter another of our short seasons and we've got to be ready. I was describing my neurotically seasonal life to a guy from Georgia and he stopped me in mid-sentence: "Y'all musta been dropped on your head once upon a time!" I laughed and explained that Vermonters do what needs to be done, crazy or not. We just keep plodding through the weather and the circumstances — reminds me of my great uncle Ira Morse who fell out of a tree one time. Although he didn't land on his head, unfortunately the fall broke his back and Uncle Ira never walked again. While it was an apple tree he fell from, fruit of another kind accompanied his fall; Uncle Ira had been suddenly and violently handed a pile of lemons, from which he chose to make the sweetest lemonade for the remainder of his life.

Ira Morse, the youngest of four boys, was as fascinated with the farm's field work as he was turned off by work inside the barn. When his oldest brother, John, was just twelve, their father got sick and had to suddenly retire. The boys were left to run the farm in Calais, Vermont, ready or not. One time John caught Ira staring from the barn out to the greenness of the back pasture. "You're supposed to be learnin' how to milk, young man!" he chided. Ira, five years old and mesmerized by the natural world, replied, "I won't ever to be tied to a cow's tail!"

The Morse brothers formed a partnership when they were old enough but Ira never warmed up to the cows. He stayed on, however, eventually marrying Eva Davis and starting a family. When that fateful tumble came, they had four children and their youngest was five. I recently talked with his boys, George and Wayne, about the accident. It was in the fall of the year and Ira was up in the tree shaking fruit onto the ground. All of a sudden a branch, weakened by the huge apple crop that year, broke and Ira came tumbling down. Before the day was over, Ira Morse was to both learn he'd never walk again, and announce that no one was to feel sorry for him — life would go on.

I don't mean to suggest that accidents are ever good, but Uncle Ira seemed to blossom from that day on. He spent the winter in bed recuperating, but spring brought a decision to break from the Morse partnership and to leap, full steam ahead, into the plant business. One of the first things he did was to gather up a small pile of barn hinges, springs and angle irons, and take his truck down to Johnny Gitchell's welding shop. He, a driver without legs and Johnny, an ace welder, put their heads together to fabricate the first of several hand-controlled vehicles that Ira would drive. Ira and Eva built, with the help of their family, a large greenhouse right next to the Morse Brothers' dairy barn. No ordinary greenhouse, it was more an ingenious patch of heaven created by a winter's pondering and an attitude that said, "can't never worked for anyone." The heating plant was fashioned from the front of a retired maple sugaring arch and some fancy brick work. Ira designed a forced-draft system where smoke from forty cords of wood was channeled through stove pipes under the plant benches; he knew that soil temperature was the most important part of greenhouse heating.

My greatest memory of Uncle Ira is of him working in the flowerbed just outside his greenhouse. It was a beautiful day in late April and the Morse Greenhouse stood backdrop to a pond that was fed by a nearby brook. Ira had manipulated the brook's route so that it passed under a fieldstone archway and over a perfect little waterfall, but nothing looked manipulated. My family and I approached Uncle Ira who sat in the soft dirt, working it with a handmade trowel. Within his reach were two aluminum crutches and a tray full of pansies he was about to plant. His dungarees were tattered and dusty from the soil and when he moved he pulled himself along with long, muscular arms.

"Mornin'," he said, smiling radiantly like the pansies. "Thanks for comin' up — come on in, I've got something to show you." He reached for his crutches and pulled himself up. We followed him into a wood framed "head house" where a mish-mash of potting material sat close to a 1950s crank cash register. He led us toward the main greenhouse and there, dug into the ground, was an area that hosted a reclining wooden office chair and various personal items.

"This is my new office," he said, beaming. The atmosphere was enhanced by 10,000 fragrant blossoms, and in the words of my cousin, Rebecca Morse, "was warm from the heat of the [sugaring] arch and it was private, for he was almost within the earth itself."

Indeed, Ira Morse was meant to be close to the earth. He often strayed into the Calais/East Montpelier countryside planting daffodils and ever-green trees, Johnny Appleseed style. He died over forty years ago but those plantings still stand as living memorials to the man who spread his wings when life had denied him legs. I was just a teenager when he died, but I'll always remember Ira Morse for building a piece of heaven on earth and making lemonade from an apple tree.

Chapter 11

Farmers' Hands

I JUST GOT BACK from being on the "Mark Johnson Show," a Vermont radio talk show concerned with everything from potholes to politics. I was part of a panel that consisted of Rob Howe, an organic dairy farmer, John O'Brien, a sheep farmer/moviemaker, and me, a maple/agri-tourism operator. Our panel was to occupy the first hour of Mark's show on the subject of "The Future of Vermont Agriculture." The second hour was to be the first of several debates between our two congressional candidates. I've always felt that agriculture is kind of the end result of politics: we're the blokes out in the field who either thrive or suffer from the affects of the strings pulled in Washington and Montpelier.

Mark started with a question about organic dairy farming, a niche that has resulted not only from folks' quest for healthier food, but also desperation in the ranks of dairy farmers. Traditional dairy farmers are being paid the same prices for their milk as they were in the 1960s, which is causing a huge frown on the face of Vermont's country landscape these days. He then went on to question the sheep farmer/moviemaker and found that wool prices are the same today as they were back in the Civil War!

Mark turned to me next, bent on finding out why a farmer would engage in such diversity as maintaining a cross-country ski center and talkin' to tourists. I told him that I had milked my share of cows, pulled my share of weeds, and paid my share of taxes. Just like Rob and John, I was simply exercising my Vermont right to creativity in farming in today's world. At one point Mark asked me if I considered myself a farmer and my answer was "Yes!", instantaneously and emphatically, like I had been asked if I was human. Of course I'm a farmer. A farmer is a farmer for life, wears it like a badge and carries it in his genes. This brings to mind an interesting story.

I had joined the Vermont National Guard's 40th Army Band and was in basic training at Fort Dix, New Jersey, back in 1969. It was the Vietnam era and I preferred to perform my duty behind a tenor trombone instead of an M-16, but I still had to attend regular infantry basic training. It was mid-summer and Fort Dix, like all army bases, was a moonscape of sand and olive drab—hot as Hades. One time we were hauled to the rifle range in windowless trailers, elbow to elbow, rifle to rifle. When we got there, they herded us out like cattle and hurried us into formation. The drill sergeant barked in a thick Puerto Rican accent, stressing the rules for safety and survival. We were finally paired off and sent to the firing points. My partner, a lanky lad whom I had not met before, looked like he grew up shootin' varmits.

"Name's Fortus. Ah want you coach me good 'case ah end up in 'Nam." His accent was southern, but also strangely reminiscent of the French Canadian back home in Vermont.

I thought of my secure army band future with a tinge of guilt and said I'd do my best. The drill sergeant barked us through several standing and kneeling firing postions:

"Ees anybaudy down range? Ees anybaudy down range? Ready on da leff? Ready on da right? Commenss firing!"

We fired at human-shaped silhouettes until the last echo sounded from the hills. After a safety check we were told to approach our targets. On our last walk to the targets, my partner spoke in a soft voice, "Ah see you a fahmah, too."

"Yeh, I am. How do you tell?"

"You have hanes of a fahmah."

I looked down at my farmer hands with pride, and told him I was a maple sugarmaker from Vermont and also raised beef cows and vegetables.

"We in da day-ree bidness down in Lou-sanna," he said. "You can allus tell a fahmah from da hanes."

Fortus and I remained friends through the rest of basic training. On the last day we said goodbye and went our separate ways. I'll always remember him and have wondered many times if he ended up in Southeast Asia. If he did, I'm sure he went with a determination to get the job done and return home to milk cows in Louisiana.

At the end of our hour on the "Mark Johnson Show," our panel made way for the politicians' segment. We left the two to debate worldly matters until November 7. After that, one will go to Washington and the other will continue the job search. I wish the victor well, but respectfully doubt that any vote he casts will turn magic for farmers. We farmers don't look toward Washington or Montpelier for serious solutions — we look out the back door at the rolling countryside, think about what makes sense, and then put our farmers' hands to work.

Chapter 12

Goin' Home

WE'VE RECENTLY WITNESSED the mass migration of folks goin' home for the holidays. Airport hysteria and late trains be damned, people's homing instinct is strong this time of year. We humans call the place we end up a home and if we're real lucky, there's a roaring fire in the wood stove and a cat purring on a rug close by. Being human, it's easy to "think in the box," but there's a whole world full of other creatures out there goin' home, too. I'd like to share stories about two of those creatures, well...three to be exact.

Yesterday there was a daddy longlegs stranded in the bottom of my tub. "Poor guy," I thought, stopping short of reaching down and helping out. He struggled up the porcelain surface only to be rebuffed time and time again by its steepness and lack of traction. I walked away afraid that any attempt to help him would harm those fragile-looking legs. Later on, when I went back to have my bath, the guy had somehow successfully climbed out and was suspended midway up the bathroom wall. He sat and watched as I drew my bath water and settled into its comfort, seemingly fixed on the huge pink creature that was occupying the place where he had recently been trapped.

Halfway through my bath, Mr. Legs decided he'd head home and I wasn't about to miss finding out where he lived. He moved easily on the dragline he had set and slowly navigated toward the ceiling. Following his apparent path, my eye came across a crack the width of a dull pencil point between the molding and the ceramic tile. I wondered which way he'd go when he got to the ceiling, but I never found out; when he reached the crack, like a strand of spaghetti sucking into puckered lips, he magically disappeared. Somehow that tangle of legs turned to rubber and Mr. Legs was home again, behind that molding which hides a whole maze of bigger cracks.

My grandmother once told me a story of another creature going home, this time with much less ease than daddy longlegs. She said her father,

Irvin Robinson, was not always kind to her and her five sisters. He wanted a son and became more curmudgeonly with the birth of each additional daughter. One time, the neighbor's bull had to be returned and Irvin had given the task to his daughter Minnie. His wife, however, sensed danger and refused to let Minnie go. Grandma said her husband whipped the girl across her leg before he left, disgruntled, to return the bull himself.

The family watched as he headed out across the pasture leading the bull by rope and halter, no doubt thankful to have him out of their hair for a while. Little did they know that his departure would almost be permanent. The neighbor's place was about a half mile away, down a steep hill through both pasture and woods. When he got within a stone's throw of the woods line, the bull made a slight "postponement" in the trip home. He suddenly knocked Irvin down and rolled him over and over, like a pine log. Irvin ended up in a ditch twenty feet from a stone wall as the bull retreated a short distance away to snort, paw the ground, and plan its next attack. Great-grandpa cowered in the ditch, no doubt thinking his days were numbered, when the beast came at him again. In one final attempt at survival, Irvin Robinson grabbed the bull's tail as it passed over him. The whipping action propelled him to the wall where he grabbed a stone and stunned the animal with a swift blow on the head.

My grandmother said her father was all battered up when he returned home and that he spent months nursing fractured ribs and sore muscles. She expressed great relief that Minnie wasn't the one to get mauled.

I asked her if they disposed of the bull. "Oh, gracious no!" she exclaimed. "That bull was just doin' what came natural to him. It took several men to finally catch him and return him home. He went on to be a great service bull. It was my father who was wrong...shouldn't a trusted the cuss!"

She said that her father's attitude toward his daughters changed for the better after that brush with death. He still gave them every dirty job the farm offered, but if he sensed any danger, he'd do the job himself.

Yes, the world is full of creatures with homes. The three you've just heard about finally did get there but not without problems along the way. Whether it's a slippery slope, a bullish attitude, or a lesson to learn, they all ended up home, blessed home...right where they belonged.

Chapter 13

Horse and Buggy Words

GOL DANG that slang! Yup, that's what we say when we're plum fed up with all the four- letter words and human expressions that get bantered about, overused, misused, and mistaken for something worthwhile. My wife and I are both Vermonters with roots as old as the hills and we prefer the words that our grandparents used. She suggested the other day that I write a column on the subject and I thought that sounded like just the cat's meow, speaking of an aging expression.

My Grandpa Morse oft used that term, "the cat's meow" to mean something that's good and appropriate. I always thought it was great to credit kitty-cats with so much good stuff, in view of all the expressions that are demeaning to animals like "pig headed, slice of the squeal, shoot the bull, grease monkey, and snake-in-the-grass." Modern words just don't have the ring to them like the ones our grandparents used. Betsy's grandmother used the word, "hark" to mean "listen" or "keep still." We never hear "hark" any more but we sure hear "shaahd up" and the kinder but more obnoxious "shshshsh," executed through O-shaped lips and an upright index finger. My grandmother had a whole library of words and phrases like "mercy, get along with you" and "for land sakes." I wasn't wild about "mercy" because it sounded like she was begging and I hated "get along with you" because it always meant I had done something wrong and she wanted me outa there. When she said "for land sakes," though, I knew she was surprised in a good way, like when I'd say, "Grandma, I got all A's on my report card," and she'd say, "For land sakes!" and then give me fresh baked cookies and a glass of milk.

The other day I was called on the carpet for using one of my Grandpa Morse's words. A woman phoned in a mail order and in my response, I used a term that had lay dormant in my brain since the days Grandpa and I worked together. I said we'd be glad to send her order out after Wendy, my mail order striker, returned on Thursday. "Striker?" the woman said, suddenly no longer interested in mail order. "What do you mean, 'striker'?" she asked in an almost chiding tone.

I gathered myself and recalled the day Grandpa and I were down in the lower pasture pounding fence posts. First, he had me punch an iron bar in the heavy soil and swivel it back and forth to expand the hole. I punched and swiveled repeatedly until the hole was big enough around and deep enough to accommodate the fence post. He then had me plunk the post into the hole and hold it while he drove it with a 20-pound, cast-iron post maul, inches from the top of my head. My grandpa was one of the few people I would have trusted to do that! It was that day that Grandpa Morse told me what a striker was.

"Burr," he said, "normally I would have been the one holding that post but you're not quite experienced enough to pound." He went on to say that usually the farmer (the boss) held the post while the hired man did the pounding, because the pounding was the hardest part of the job. To do that, however, the farmer had to trust the hired man with his life. According to Grandpa, a "striker" is any employee who is skilled and trustworthy—don't expect Webster to agree, but what does Webster know compared to a Vermont farmer!

I told the "striker" story to the lady on the phone and she allowed that both the word and the work ethic are obsolete! She went on to place the order, convinced that I was not demeaning anyone on my mail-order staff. "On the contrary," I said, "I've got a wonderful staff and find them all loyal, skilled, and trustworthy." We went on to discuss the weather and politics and seemed like old friends at the end. Just before she hung up, she asked if I would trust Wendy with a twenty-pound post maul. I thought of the petite, blond Wendy and visualized myself, hands grasping the top of a cedar fence post, cringing at the rhythmic thunk, thunk, thunk just inches from my head. I ended the phone call that day by using another expression we rarely hear these days: "Not by a damned sight!"

My problem with modern-day expressions is that many times, they're either too trite or too unprintable. If the spoken word, however, truly reflects the character or eccentricity of a person, it's OK with me, off-color or not. I've got a neighbor who prefaces just about everything he says with, "As the sayin' goes." He's a true character, smart as a whip, and honorable as all get-out, and I respect his creativity with the English language. He also sneaks in an occasional "b' guess and b'gory" and " a-hankerin' to." Yup, brings me right back to the good ol' days, as the sayin' goes, or, more accurately, "as the sayin' went."

Chapter 14

House Cleaning and Presidents

IT HAS BEEN ALMOST a year now since my mother left to be with my father up in the great beyond. My siblings and I have been slow to empty and clean their house, probably to avoid the feeling of "finality." There's nothing, however, more depressing than a house sitting empty through a Vermont winter, and recent frosty nights have gently tapped us on the shoulder with the message, "get that place ready and find someone to move in." Last weekend the spirit moved, literally; we felt Dot and Harry Morse guiding us from room to room.

The four of us, plus my good wife Betsy, met with an array of pickup trucks, cleaning utensils, and cardboard boxes. We knew that decisions would be more of the personal nature than monetary because Harry and Dot Morse were not "material" people. What they left was family memorabilia—tons of it, which required our attention, piece by dusty piece. We pawed through messages like "To SuziQ on your fifth birthday," and all our report cards from the first grade on. My biggest find, however, was a legal pad with notes I had gathered on a 1971 visit to my Grandpa and Grandma Morse. I had long since forgotten them, but the notes revealed my interest in their stories for a book I wanted to write some day. The book, which miraculously happened over thirty years later, contained material not on the long-forgotten legal pad. Now I have a gold mine of stories to take me well into the future, right from Grandpa and Grandma's mouths!

All five of us found things we considered more valuable than diamond tiaras or gold coins. The biggest "family" find, however, was this 1960 letter written to my grandparents:

> *Dear Mr. and Mrs. Morse:*
> *A group of high school students from Montpelier left with Senator Prouty, who delivered it to me, a gallon of the justly famous Vermont maple syrup. I understand you were good enough to give the syrup to the group, and this note*

brings to you my warm and personal thanks for your kindness.
With best wishes,
Dwight Eisenhower

It was on White House stationary and the signature was the real thing!

Finding that Eisenhower letter reminds me of another "presidential" experience: I drove up to my neighbor Bradford Lane's place a while back to pick his fertile, Vermont brain for stories. He met me at the door, looking all his eighty-something years, and led me into the living room he shares with his wife Ruth. I was immediately drawn to an old photo of a man in a three-piece suit.

"Know who that is?" he asked.

"Calvin Coolidge," I said, without hesitation.

Bradford chuckled, like only Bradford Lane can, and invited me to sit down. It seems the photo was of his father, Homer Lane, who was a spitting image of Calvin Coolidge. He and Ruth had recently found the old photo and put it out for display. He explained that a Lane neighbor had been invited to the Coolidge White House once with her 4-H club to cook a Thanksgiving turkey for the President. While there, she told Mr. Coolidge about her neighbor back in Vermont, who "favored" the President. When she returned to Vermont, she told Mrs. Lane that the President wanted a picture of Homer Lane. Bradford said his mother tried every trick in the book to get her workaholic husband into a business suit. Mr. Lane scoffed at coming in from the fields for such foolishness but finally complied, complete with a perfect "Calvin Coolidge" frown! Bradford pointed to a place where work clothes peeked beyond the fringes of the business suit. He said his father made "short work" of shedding that fancy outer layer when the photographer finished.

Sadly, the days are gone when common folks get personal letters from presidents, or are invited to cook them turkeys. Oh yes, times have changed —we don't get "silent" presidents anymore and presidential look-alikes flock, for big bucks, to late-night talk shows, not farmhouse living rooms. And speakin' of big bucks, I'd never send a whole gallon of maple syrup to a president—maybe a pint but never a whole gallon! There are a few times, however, when the spirit of simpler times is close at hand, like that weekend we cleaned. We finally got the old house livable again and last night, for the first time in almost a year, the lights of its new inhabitants shone brightly. It looks happy once again.

Chapter 15

Legislative Lunacy

IT'S A SPRINGTIME ritual here in Vermont. As fledgling buds appear on the trees, the last steamy gasp rises into an atmosphere full of talk about the departing season—and I don't mean maple sugarin'—I'm talking about Vermont's other steamy institution, the legislature. Yup, the solons here in Vermont just pulled up stakes and left camp for 2006. They departed to the usual chorus of praise, put-downs, and the "lateness of the hour," but I say "pshaw" to that: there was once a session that went right into August —oh yes, I know because I was there as a page boy.

It was 1961 and I remember the excitement of being selected as one of twelve boys to serve from January till the session's end. We attended our regular schools on Mondays to receive a week's worth of homework. Our peers looked upon us as the "dandy dozen" because we wore coats and ties and didn't have to attend school, but there was nothing special about us —we were boys through and through! Because the powers that be recognized this, we were all required to have a close relation who worked at or served in the legislature. My grandpa, Sidney Morse, was representing the town of East Montpelier in that session. Deep respect for him kept my deviltry at bay —that is till the session crept into the heat of mid-summer when tempers flared and neckties were poison to boys.

It all started one cold day in January when Grandpa and I drove the three miles from our farm in his '57 Chrysler. I was having second thoughts about the "honor" of it all when we walked through the hallowed hallways on our way to meet our counterparts. His were 240 other representatives from every city and town in Vermont and mine were eleven boys with fresh haircuts and clean ears. We shook hands and exchanged pleasantries on day one, like the adults. Day two brought orientation and relegation of jobs and by day three we had "mixed it up" with a few dirty jokes and shoulder punches; we were best friends, a band of hellions bent on using the inner bowels of the Vermont Statehouse for both workplace and playground.

In our free time we sought out the more interesting staff—custodians, legislative draftsmen, and good-looking secretaries. One secretary was an older woman who seemed suspicious of us. She sat at her desk, chain-smoking much of the time; her abrasive attitude begged retaliation from our band of twelve. One day a page named Jimmy brought in a cigarette load which, he said in a hushed tone, "had her name written on it." We knew that when she took her bathroom breaks, she left her cigarettes lying on her desk next to the overflowing ashtray. We waited, and when the time came, Jimmy slipped in and inserted that load into one of her cigarettes. I was on duty in the general area of her office when she lit the loaded one. Her shriek resounded through the hallways and I rushed to join a group congregating at her door. Squirming my way to the front, I peered through the blue haze into her office where she sat spitting mad. Whiskers of dirty cigarette residue sprouted from her eyebrows down to her pointed chin, but it was sterile clean compared with the words coming from her mouth!

We managed to cover up our role in the cigarette caper, but there was another time two of us got caught red-handed in some mischief that wasn't even of our making. The 1961 legislature was desperately dysfunctional, just the wrong mixture of personalities and political persuasions. Those folks had good intentions, I'm sure, but their ability to make mountains into molehills was astounding; they couldn't legislate their way out of a wet paper bag and that became more obvious as June and July turned to August. There was, however, a group down there that was even less upstanding than the legislature—the press corps. One day when the heat was unbearable in the House Chamber and the session's end had been hovering for days, a particularly notorious reporter approached a couple of us page boys. He brought us into a huddle like a thug offering a deal on gold watches.

"Hey, you guys wanna be on television?" he asked, knowing we couldn't pass up an opportunity like that.

He had made a huge banner that said "Solons Go Home!" and asked us to approach the Speaker's podium with it in front of the entire General Assembly. Since he was an adult, we felt obliged to honor his request, plus it seemed like an interesting task. We gathered at the doorkeeper's station and at the reporter's signal, proudly started our march toward the Speaker of the House. Half way down the aisle, the Speaker's face turned beet red.

We knew we had been duped when he angrily motioned us to the sidelines. Soon we both received a curt message to report to the office of the Speaker of the House.

Needless to say we got "lined out in lavender" by Mr. Speaker. It was impossible to break into his tirade and we finally gave up trying. When he finished, we offered a weak apology and never did divulge the real culprit. The 1961 session ended later that day, and Grandpa Morse and I wasted no time in heading home. As we got in the Chrysler, I started to apologize to him about the events earlier in the day but Grandpa Morse, the wisest man in the world, brushed off my apology:

"Burr," he said. "I know it was that crackpot reporter who put you up to it and I'm sure you caught hell from the Speaker of the House." He went on to say the reporter needed learn the difference between work and play, a mission that could be best accomplished on a farm, wielding a dung fork! His next advice, however, required an eyewink:

"Don't let that Speaker bother you — no one listened to him all session so why should you start now?"

Chapter 16

Milkin' Cows and Messy Meetings

BEING A LIFETIME farmer, I've seen my share of terra firma close up. In fact sometimes it seems farmers attract miscellaneous scuz by osmosis or, if you will, "scuzmosis." The other day I was at a meeting of the Vermont Attractions Association held at beautiful St. Anne's Shrine on the shore of Lake Champlain. I'm not that good at meetings but I maintained reasonable dignity through the first part. After a while, though, I'd had my fill of Robert's Rules and began fidgeting in my seat. My eyes navigated the large conference room looking for things to count and interesting pictures. I fixed for a time on a distant wall clock that said 10:45 and didn't seem to move. Huge windows surround the hall and would have promised a panoramic view of the lake had the day not been drizzly and grey. We'd received a large stack of handouts before the meeting and I was intently doodling on them when my eyes strayed to the floor. I was horrified to see my well-worn sneakers rising out of enough grass clippings and hay chaff to support a small cow. "What the?" I thought, hoping it was a common problem. To my horror, however, sideways glances at my neighbors' feet showed complete tidiness. Adding insult to injury, Duane Marsh, head of the Vermont Chamber of Commerce, sported spit-polished shoes that would have passed muster in anyone's army. He sat right beside me and the contrast was shattering. I was attempting to discreetly scuff the stuff into a single pile when I noticed the clippings had somehow migrated to the woman in front of me. The stuff had not only worked its way under her chair, but up onto her suede blazer which hung neatly on the back of her chair. It looked like she'd just had a roll in the hay. My mind was made up: if she started scratching behind her ears, I was getting out of there!

Finally, the clock said 12:15 and Robert's unwritten rule, hunger, adjourned the meeting. We all rose, stretched and turned to our neighbors for small talk. Duane and I shook hands and then I cut right to the chase; I knew that we were both thinking about that mess on the floor.

"Duane," I said, sheepishly, "I don't know where I picked all that stuff up. I'm embarrassed about the mess but..."

He interrupted me with a wave of his hand and then said something really surprising, even complimentary in a round-about way:

"Don't worry about it, Burr." He continued, glancing down at his spit-polished shoes. "I've always kinda wished I could be more like you."

We were swept into the food line before he could elaborate, but I have a theory about what Duane meant: You see, in one way or another, everyone wants to be a farmer. There's a perception out there that a farmer is his own boss and has no constraints over appearance, talk or habits, things that cause considerable grief in the non-farm world. Duane's a diplomat by trade, so to speak, and certainly plied his trade that day; he made me feel OK; in fact, important for carrying the gene for "scuzmosis."

I'm reminded of another time someone forgave my sloppiness; this time, a farmer. I was doing chores for Gerald Pease while he vacationed. On the final milking I found a huge Holstein had calved a short distance from the barn. I went and got Gerald's wheelbarrow, hefted the calf in, and escorted mother and daughter back to the barn. The cow's udder was so flush with milk it looked like it was about to explode. I left her to milk last, knowing her milk must not be mixed with the saleable milk. When I finally got to her, I massaged her udder with a damp cloth and the milk started streaming out before I applied the four teat cups. While I waited for her to milk out, I examined the newborn calf, pondering how to coax some of that mother's milk into her. When the udder looked shrunken and felt limp, I released the vacuum and removed the teat cups. A torrent of milk drained from the cups and tubes leading to the vacuum system, drenching my shoes. I wondered, fleetingly, where milk goes once the machine is full, but didn't think any more of it until I was talking to Gerald a few weeks later.

"You know that big Holstein that freshened when you were gone, Gerald?" I said, proud that I had cared for the calf and overseen the mother's first milking.

"Yup."

"Well, she gave more than a milking machine full."

"I know," he said, training his eyes on mine but speaking through a wide, forgiving grin."Milk went right back through the piping to the vacuum pump...got a bacteria count of two million...dairy threatened to shut me down!"

He went on to explain that I should have flushed out the entire system with sanitizer, that milk doesn't simply evaporate into thin air, and rotting milk is the farmer's enemy. He was careful to assure me, however, the situation was finally resolved and that he knew my intentions were good. I left that day feeling relieved that Gerald, like Duane, had accepted my lot in life: I try my best, work hard, and, yes, carry the gene for "scuzmosis." I can't help it — I'm a farmer.

Chapter 17

Old Rugged Crossroads

"Egad, they must be wicked desperate!" Those were my exact words when the idea was first broached about preaching at Adamant Methodist Church. I'm not, mind you, suggesting that the words "wicked" or "desperate" apply to the Adamant Methodist Church, or that I refused their offer. I did indeed guest preach there the other day. In a weird sort of way it felt like going home again. You see, Adamant Methodist Church was where my feeble beginnings and unfortunate endings as a churchgoer happened. I've always been a believer but we were farm people with a seven-day excuse. We lived clean, practiced honesty — figured we were earning our passage to heaven by milking cows and hefting bales, by God! The few times my family did attend church were at Adamant Methodist and for some strange reason that tiny church will forever be etched in my mind as "the little church that could." I felt both honored and a bit hypocritical to step behind its simple pulpit the other day, but was warmly welcomed by this generation of Adamant's faithful.

Adamant, the community, is a bit like a scarred-up old mongrel. Its geographic makeup is 3/4 Calais and 1/4 East Montpelier. It has seen many a fight and has a questionable reputation. In fact the village was once so rough and tumble that it was originally called Sodom. Sodom, Vermont, was home to Wicked Pond and a genetically questionable bunch of Sodomites (or as my father used to call them, "Sodom-o-cranes") whose purpose in life was to live fast and quarry from the huge granite cache underfoot in Sodom. No one seems to know when Sodom became Adamant, but the transition is an obvious result of kinder and gentler times. The granite industry pulled up stakes in the early 1900s and left the area pocked with gaping holes, rusting machinery, and a gentler society— exit Sodom, enter Adamant. Webster defines the word "adamant" as "an unbreakable or extremely hard substance," words that fit Adamant, Vermont, like a well-worn quarrier's glove.

The Adamant of my youth was a village in transition. It consisted of an ancient co-op store, a tiny church, and a handful of well-worn houses at a junction of five gravel roads. The houses fit awkwardly beside a brook connecting an upper and lower pond. I remember one place close to the junction that had an open drainpipe protruding from its second floor. An elderly woman lived in the house and that pipe discharged, in sync with nature's call, into the swampy edge of Wicked Pond. Just up the road from the store was a large wooden structure that has been key to the evolution of Adamant. In Sodom's heyday it served as a dance hall. For a while it was cleared out Sunday mornings for church service. Sodom's attitude, however, held firmly for "separation of church and dance hall"; eventually an old store was moved onto a new foundation just up the road from the dance hall and stands, to this day, as the Adamant Methodist Church.

When I was a boy, the dance hall building had become the Adamant School of Music, a fledgling summer school for piano students. It drew scorn from many of the locals who cited the New York City teachers as "long-hairs or Communists." At first they were discouraged from populating the old dance hall, much like church services had previously been. The Adamant School of Music somehow survived, however, and currently enjoys worldwide recognition. A piano-tuner friend recently told me that there are about fifty grand pianos today in Adamant, Vermont. Most of them are Steinways — several reside in Barney Hall, the place that was too much a dance hall to be either a church or a music school! Adamant's entire personality, in fact, has changed lately, thanks to a few folks of means who have moved to the village and taken it under their wing. These days the brook exits the upper pond via a resurrected milldam and veritably dances to the lower pond over stoned-up waterfalls and picturesque pools. The village houses sport new coats of paint and lend Stowe-class charm to theater performances, world-class concerts, artist studios and the annual Black Fly Festival, complete with a blood drawing from the Red Cross!

Except for some minor stumbling and a total void of fire and brimstone, my sermon about unconditional love went well that day. At the end we all shook hands and exchanged pleasantries, guided by that love, and then I went down to the Adamant Co-op, America's oldest co-op store. I bought a soda pop and strolled across the road to enjoy it by the brook. As the ancient water danced by, I could hear the sounds of derricks straining to lift huge chunks of granite, Sodom's drunken brawls, and gentle hymns sung by struggling congregations. The water spoke of preachers who farm, farmers who preach, musicians, thespians, Flatlanders and vintage Vermonters. It embraced both the peaceful and the ugly; the water is the history book and today's Adamant is but one chapter, softer and gentler, but very unbreakable.

Chapter 18

Party Pooper by Training

"Go Solons!" That was our school chant but I rarely participated. We were the Montpelier High School Solons and I, frankly, questioned the hoopla of it all. I went there in 1962, a painfully shy, round-faced alumnus of eight years in East Montpelier one-room schoolhouses. Except for band and English Comp, in fact, I spent most of my four years there being as invisible as a boy could be. Our fortieth class reunion was recently held — you guessed it, without me. I was encouraged to go by a few classmates but declined; "No" I said. "Why should I suddenly become a joiner?"

The other night as I was heading toward Burlington, I noticed several huge tents of Circus Smirkus on the grounds of Montpelier High School — reminded me of an experience long before my tenure there — in fact, before the high school had even been built. It was the middle of summer and one night, after a grueling day in the hayfields, my father announced that we were going to the circus. By the time we finished the evening milking, ate supper, and cleaned up, it was about dusk. I sensed it was late for the circus as my mother, father, sister Susie, and I headed down the road. When we got to the future site of Montpelier High School, Dad pulled the family DeSoto to the side of the road and shut off the engine. "Where's the circus?" I asked, seeing nothing but shadowy figures out in the field. "Right out there," Dad said, pointing to the shadowy figures. "And you're going to see the best part of the circus, the setting up." His enthusiasm was great enough to squelch any disappointment Susie or I might have felt and when we cranked down the windows, the excitement truly did begin.

The field was bustling with activity under temporary floodlights. A generator hummed in the background and swirling mist crept up from the river, adding a surreal effect to the scene. My father's excited narration kept us as spellbound as any seasoned ringmaster would have. "The performers — midgets, musclemen, and bearded ladies — all have to set up the circus," he said, "and if you look close you can pick them out!" Susie and I stared wide-eyed, imagining the personalities behind the hammering and heft-ing. As we watched, we munched on popcorn our mother had made and drank from a jug of homemade root beer. Our biggest thrill came when the elephants appeared as huge black forms in the night. They carried and towed things in slow motion, each guided by a keeper and a few strategic cuss words. Finally the huge big top rose up and just as it peaked, a thick fog swallowed up our show and it was time to go home. We crept home through the fog, ready to let dreams of the "Greatest Show on Earth" top off the evening.

Another time we packed a picnic lunch, donned our high boots, and headed toward a special swamp where pitcher plants grew. We walked through a dark, deciduous woods while Dad told us about different kinds of ferns and "shushed" us occasionally to point out wild animals. The black flies got worse as we went deeper into the woods, but Dad brushed aside our complaints saying, "Everything has a purpose." When we reached the edge of the swamp, he beckoned toward a shady spot and we began slog-ging toward it, our steps making sucking sounds. "There's some," he said, pointing to a mat of vegetation on the swamp floor. He used the word "carnivorous" as we knelt down to examine plants that had leafy apertures lined with spiny tendrils. They looked like regular old plants to Susie and me but to Dad, they were specimens supreme. "Shhh," he whispered. "See that fly light on one of 'em?" Before our eyes, the pleasant-looking plant became a grinning murderer as the aperture closed and swallowed the fly — everything has a purpose.

Yes, my father was that way — he always wanted us to know about things "behind the scene." I've thought about our fortieth class reunion and won-dered if I made a mistake by not going. I do hold a certain curiosity about where life has taken my classmates and I wish them nothing but the best. For the time being, however, I'll accept my upbringing; I was trained by a very wise man that the main attraction is not always the best part of the show and, by golly, if that fly the pitcher plant ate could talk I bet he'd agree!

Chapter 19

Singin' and Sawin'

I SIT AT MY COMPUTER, pondering my next column. The November view of my favorite valley lies beyond the window to my left, somehow tempting me. I dwell on the surrounding walls and the log floor joists and board sub-floor above my head. I think of that lumber, how every stick in those walls and ceiling were sawed by Carroll Badger, the guy across the valley. The valley. The boards. Memories come back of Carroll's old Lane sawmill singing across the valley. It was powered by a Cadillac V8 engine that roared as the huge circular saw blade ripped through logs. Filtered by the valley, though, the roaring and ripping was tamed to soothing music by the time it reached our place. My fingers suddenly attack the keyboard— Carroll Badger'll be my subject this week.

When I was younger, we never bought any lumber for building projects around the farm. We went to the woods, cut trees, and hauled the logs over to Carroll's mill. Carroll sawed in a dilapidated lean-to built into the side hill where logs would spill, easily, onto a runway. He manipulated them, down grade, onto the mill's carriage with a peevee. Over the years dozens of folks offered to help with the sawing but Carroll always insisted on working alone. He told a story about how that very mill sliced a man in half once before he got it and he didn't want that to happen again. That was his excuse for working alone but I knew the real reason: Carroll required absolute order in his life. He got up each morning, figured a plan for the day, and worked on his own schedule. Doing it any other way would have been as awkward for Carroll Badger as rollin' a log uphill without a peevee.

He was a small, gentle man who wore the same cap all the years that I knew him. He only went away once that I knew of and that was to the war. When he returned, it was to the farm across the valley. That's where he stayed —never even traveled to New Hampshire that I knew. Some folks thought of Carroll as a "putterer," but not me. Carroll Badger was both "Jack" and "Master" of any trade he ever tackled. The sawmill was just one of the odds and ends that supplied his livelihood. He hayed, sugared, cut wood, drove the school bus, played music, baked cookies—Carroll was an intellectual switch-hitter; both sides of his brain worked equally well.

I guess it was his left brain, the side in charge of orderliness, that found him out in the mill workin' alone. It also found him religiously greasing, oiling, and fine-tuning the multi-motorized contraptions on his farm. That same left brain took him to town one day a week, driving an ancient vehicle, and checking off a well-thought-out list. Town was only a three-mile drive but a return for something forgotten was out of the question for Carroll. The Badger house was an uninsulated hulk of a place and Carroll lived alone in the kitchen and one adjoining room. He had a wood cook stove that heated his water and cranked out delectables both winter and summer. He was so frugal that the power company periodically investigated him for hot-wiring—they couldn't understand why his bill was $6.00 when all the neighbors were paying $30! His frugality never kept him from handing out those delectables all over the neighborhood though, and being a friend to all.

Carroll's un-logical side was marked by some of the contraptions he fabricated and impulsive things he did. He was always tinkering in his shop with welders, drill presses, and acetylene torches. One time he made the weirdest doodlebug (for those who don't know, a doodlebug is a homemade tractor, fabricated from old car parts and miscellaneous farm junk). He morphed the front half of a Henry-J automobile to the back half of a Fordson tractor and ended up with a machine that resembled a rocket ship with iron wheels! The remains of that thing still sit, rusting, in the woods between the Badger Place and ours. Close to that same spot was a common picnic site where we used to meet Carroll—he'd bring the hotdogs and we'd bring the beans. I remember one time we were having a sing-along over at our place. We saw a top-heavy figure approaching from way down in the valley and our speculation grew as it slowly got nearer and nearer. Finally, just as we finished one of our songs, Carroll came trudging up over the bank; he'd heard the music from his side of the valley, strapped on his accordion, and followed the music, like a beagle with its nose to the ground.

Carroll's logical side took over toward the end of his life. He sold the farm to neighbors who he knew would care for it and keep it undeveloped. He bought a small ranch house just up the road and planned to move there at a later date—or did he? One day, back in 1990, I stopped at his place to pay a saw bill. I walked straight in, past his car and through the typical New England woodshed entryway. It was a rainy day and normally he would have been in the kitchen making cookies. When he didn't respond to my knock, I knew something was wrong. As I turned to leave, I glanced further into the woodshed and there lay Carroll at the base of a partly built woodpile. His heart had simply given out a few hours before while he was piling wood, doin' what he loved. In death, as in life, Carroll's house was in order.

Chapter 20

The Center School

Last week I spent one day at the Vermont Farm Show. Although it hasn't really changed much since my toddler days, I always enjoy it. That afternoon I was drooling over a certain Bobcat skid-steer loader when I realized the guy drooling next to me was an old classmate, Bradley Witham. Bradley and I attended East Montpelier Center School once upon a time, back when all eight grades were in the same room. Most everyone in town was tied to farming in one way or another and all of us thought we wanted to be farmers when we grew up, except one. He wanted to be a "joctor" so he could help "thick" people (I never found out if he was ever thuckthessful).

It was great reminiscing with Bradley. He was in the fourth grade and I was in the first. Our teacher, Mrs. Spicer, kept all eight levels of learning in process like a juggler keeps balls in the air. Some of us, myself included, had the attention span of a flash bulb. One time she caught me molding an obscene object out of clay. I'll always remember feeling the shame wring from my six-year-old being with her single finger wag and icy stare—I've been quite well behaved ever since.

Brad reminded me that the Center School was heated by wood. He said one time the fire went out in the night. Frozen water pipes forced a postponement of the Pledge of Allegiance and the Lord's Prayer that morning. He described a hurried trip to the neighbors for dry wood and kindling— first things first! I didn't remember that episode but have vivid memories of another warming exercise—lunchtime. Back in those days, hot lunch didn't start up till winter.

Before that we all brought our own sandwiches, if we were lucky enough to have them. I remember some kids from a poor family bringing sandwiches that had a pea-green complexion—all that was left for sandwich material in their house was pickle juice! My mother always sent me to school with a perfectly adequate lunch but when the noon bell rang, I'd gravitate to my buddies, the Hill boys. Their mother's sandwiches were thick and sliced diagonally. My favorite "Hill" sandwich was tuna and crisp lettuce on generously buttered bread. It was always a great day when some creative bargaining netted me one of those glorious tuna sandwiches.

When hot lunch started in the late fall, we had to pick it up at Mrs. Wilma Anderson's house, a ways down the hill from the Center School. We had a sled with a special wooden box on it and two kids were designated each day to make the trip. I remember going one time with an older boy named Allie. One of the eighth-grade girls bundled me up and turned me over to the huge, frightening Allie. The road down to the Andersons had a packed snow surface and I remember Allie kicking off, jumping on the box, and leaving me to find my own way. I wasn't frightened because I knew the landmarks —the Old Meeting House, the Community Center, and the Paine Farm. When I got there I was fighting tears, however, more from frustration than fear of being lost. Wilma Anderson, a kind, matronly woman, comforted me with a pinch of my cheek and a warm cookie.

We made several trips to the sled with armloads of packaged rolls and accessories. The main course, a huge pot of spaghetti, made the sled heavy and hard to push back up the hill. Allie and I were friends by the time we reached the top; he even let me ride when the road leveled out. I'll always remember Wilma Anderson's spaghetti, thick with meat sauce and good old USDA surplus grated cheese!

Every time my wife, Betsy, serves spaghetti, I think of hot lunch at the Center School but I pass on the cheese these days. They say we shouldn't have stuff like that in these times of different eating habits and professions. The Center School, no doubt, cranked out more doctors than farmers in the final years before its doors closed as a school and opened as a residence. Farmers, in fact, are a rare breed today, but those of us who are left still get together once a year at the Vermont Farm Show. Oh, by the way—Bradley Witham farms just up the road from my own place. Some things just never change.

Chapter 21

Tin Pan Corners

A FEW YEARS AGO a neighbor, Bradford Lane, came to me with a message. "Burr," he said, "I read your columns in the newspaper and kinda like your way with words." He had a couple things rattlin' around in his head that he wanted me to consider writing up for posterity. I was so honored at the chance to be his historical pipeline that, after our meeting, I sat right down and wrote a couple columns on Bradford's memories. The other day I heard from him again.

This time his situation had changed. His son, Stanley, called from the Lamoille County town of Cambridge, where Bradford recently moved from his native East Montpelier. Stanley said his father now needs assistance with living; "remembers things from the past but sometimes has trouble with five minutes ago," Stanley said. That day Bradford was thinking about "Tin Pan Corners" and wanted to know if I'd ever heard the story. I immediately jumped in my car..."three-dollar gas be damned," I thought, "this can't wait."

Bradford and his wife of sixty-seven years, Ruth, now live in a ski chalet that their son, David, has converted from a horse barn. Stanley met me at the door and led me into the small, comfortable place where Bradford Lane, thinner and more stooped than the last time I had seen him, sat waiting for me. One thing that hadn't changed was his handshake; his huge, cow-milkin' hand still packed a crushing wallop! I slid a chair over close and he proceeded to tell me his story.

Bradford's farm was in the Horn of the Moon section of East Montpelier, up where Sanders Circle turns to the right toward the Horn's northwest. Just outside of Sanders Circle was the farm of Perley Sanders who Bradford and Stanley remember as a real big man. "I'm a small man," Bradford said, exposing one more thing that has not changed—a toothy, boyish grin. "In the winter time, I had to jump to match up with tracks Perley left in the snow!"

Bradford said Perley Sanders farmed, like lots of folks in that day and age, but also regularly went up into the hills trapping. Apparently persistence marked another of Perley's traits because, according to Bradford, most folks had given up trapping by that time. In back of Perley's farm is Long Meadow Hill and on the back side of Long Meadow Hill is a point where the towns of Calais, Worcester, Middlesex, and East Montpelier all come together. That is, these days there's a point; back in Perley's time, Bradford said, the point was marked by a tin pan...Perley's tin pan...and he moved it around frequently! He said folks always accepted Perley's law of "boundary by cooking utensil" until the day he died. "On that day," Bradford said, "the tin pan disappeared and folks started usin' the map!" I puzzled over why Perley moved the boundary. Bradford said he didn't know that part of the story. Was it because he was bigger than everyone else and could? Was he obsessive compulsive and just needed to move things around or was there some kind of political advantage for catching critters on certain days in certain towns? I decided to bid Bradford goodbye and try to find out more at a later date.

As I headed back toward home on VT Route 15, Sterling Range stood stark and looming on my right. Over that way, Route 108 winds through Smuggler's Notch to connect Jeffersonville and Stowe. Route 108 was built back in the olden days to accommodate vehicles small enough to navigate its steep, hairpin curves. Recently six different tractor-trailers have chosen that route over Smuggler's Notch and gotten wedged, tighter than a woodchuck in a rat hole, apparently tricked by the modern-day GPS, an instrument smart enough to pinpoint a boundary to the nearest fleck of dust, but too stupid to distinguish an eighteen-wheel Kenworth from a Subaru. I chuckled to myself at the thought..."how much better is that than Perley Sander's system?" After asking a few other Horn of the Moonites, I never found more information on Perley Sanders. Neighbor Eddie Cote, however, said this about Bradford Lane: "Bradford knew, pretty much, where everything was." That was good enough for me. I had been honored, once again, to talk to Bradford Lane, a small man who always knew his boundaries and farmed for a lifetime within them. Lately age has shrunken Bradford's boundaries but his urge to keep history alive is big, a concept that's getting scarcer than, well, tin pans these days up on Long Meadow Hill. Three cheers for Bradford Lane.

Chapter 22

A Town with Character

I WAS RECENTLY ASKED to attend a meeting of the Worcester Writers Group. Although the words "writers group" sounded a bit stuffy, I agreed to go and say a few words about my writing. On the appointed night, I drove up County Road through Maple Corner and over the hill toward Worcester. Maple Corner always feels like home to me. That's where I spent my first five years and I truly think my heart never moved. As I approached the quaint village where I was to speak, great thoughts started to flood in. Worcester was full of "characters" and jumping with lore when I grew up and, come to think of it, probably ranks second for my placement of heart. It had mink farms, sawmills, hillside farms and a farm equipment dealer—all things positive for an impressionable young tyke like me. The best thing Worcester had, though, was "characters" and I mean that in a loving sense. The average Worcester "character" is a cut above, maybe even closer to God. In this case, it's probably something in the water; after all, the stream running through Worcester is called Minister Brook.

My personal relationship with Worcester dates back to the 1970s. When work slowed down on the farm in the winter, I drove a truck for a Worcester mink farm turned rendering plant. I went to farms all over northern Vermont picking up deceased farm animals (lots of stories there but maybe not suitable right now!). More recently, I'd go over to my Uncle Bernard's machine shop across the brook from the old rendering plant. Every Friday night country musicians gathered, kitchen-junket style. They called themselves the Broken String Band but played healthy string music amongst the metal lathes, scrap piles, and ailing bucket loaders. I'd usually leave with a beer in my belly and always with a great appreciation for those wonderful sounds.

When I got to the church where the writers' event was to be held, I parked, grabbed my notes, and headed in to the back meeting hall. My fear disappeared quicker than a Worcester mink when the first person I saw was my good friend Wayne Richardson. I used to ride shotgun with Wayne on the rendering truck and his smiling face brought relief; I knew I would be OK. Then I started recognizing other folks in the room, including a couple of relatives. My friendly hostess shook my hand and led me to the punch and cookie table. I began to suspect the only hazard I faced was being one-upped by these writers of the Worcester old guard, a premonition that proved accurate.

My tales drew the laughs and expressions I desired. There was one guy in the audience whom I didn't recognize as Worcester old guard. He had the required double twinkle in his eye of a Worcester character, however. My repertoire included a couple stories of note: one about an old man shooting at a lily pad and another about my father helping a skunk out of a jar. As I talked I could see the man taking mental notes and somehow knew I would be hearing from him. I later learned that his name was Newell and, sure enough, Newell was suddenly on his feet in response to my skunk story. He told of a skunk, similarly stuck in a jar, but his skunk was really stuck. In my story my father lulled the skunk out of the jar simply by stroking its back and he didn't get sprayed. Newell's skunk was so badly stuck that his guy had to grab the Mason jar with one hand, the skunk's derriere with the other, and actually unscrew the skunk from the jar! Newell said the guy was halfway to the next county so fast that he never found out if Mr. Skunk sprayed. Chalk one up for Newell!

After my gun story, Newell was literally gushing with a tale about a hunter who placed his rifle on two spikes on the wall, one supporting the barrel and the other protruding through the trigger guard. As he walked away, the barrel slipped off, allowing the gun to suddenly pivot downward and discharge. That, in turn, gave it momentum to rotate for a repeat performance until the bullets were all gone. He hilariously described the hunters, frantically exiting from the gun-gone-berserk. "When they returned," he said, "the place looked like a battle zone." Chalk two up for Newell!!

I had a great time that night—heck, I always have a great time in Worcester. My worries about speaking to a group of writers were unfounded and the only "rub" was a pleasant one: being one-upped twice by a Worcester character. After all, what could I expect in a village where folklore was invented and Minister Brook flows with magic water.

Chapter 23

A Trip to the "Mall"

As THE TWILIGHT OF AUTUMN approaches and all our tour buses fade from these balding hills, I head out to remedy my sagging woodpile problem. Yes, I usually have a semblance of dry wood hangin' around but have never quite mastered the concept of cutting it all a year in advance and stacking to dry. My father used to tell of an old guy who waited till the dog's water started to freeze before he fed the fire. He'd then go out, cut a single chunk off a nearby tree, and "worry" it into sizzling flame until the next time Fido's water froze. I'm not quite that lax but do find myself out looking over the acreage for dead, slightly drier trees altogether too often.

I'm happy in the woods this time of year and feel lucky to have all the tools of a Vermont farmer: lots of forest acreage, a Husqvarna chain saw, and a serviceable tractor with a bucket loader. My Husqvarna is a true marvel of modern engineering. It'll start on the first or second pull, even with a sawdust-filled air cleaner and a three-year-old spark plug. It's so lightweight and versatile that it cuts at all angles, upside down and even at a full, one-armed stretch to dock off high limbs (I can hear gasps from all the forest purists out there!). I usually hook onto whole trees, skid them out to a level place, lift them to waist height with the bucket loader, and cut off Tootsie Roll chunks without even bending my back. Compared to the woodcutting stories of woe that my forebears told, my process is a piece of cake.

Axes and crosscut saws are notorious items of early forest torture but I'm thinking of the most notorious of all: the Mall chain saw. The Mall, a malignant brainchild of a frustrated crosscut-user, was built before chain saws made sense; the Edsel, in comparison, was a colossal success. It was hyped as a new, dynamic power saw that could be used with ease by two men. My friend, David Newhall, says it was really a four-man saw — "wore out the two men who lugged it to the woods and then took two fresh men to run it!" I'm too young to have ever run one but remember seeing the medieval thing laying around our farm. My brother Elliott, who is ten years my senior, had some personal experience with the Mall, however. He said it was brutally heavy, but damage to one's back was not the worst of Mall punishment.

"You started it by winding a rope around a pulley," he said. "It had wicked high compression and two men had to hold it down while one pulled. Sometimes we wound that rope dozens of times before it started. Sometimes the rope slipped off the pulley or it broke and I'd go ass over elbow into brush, briars, or if I was lucky, the deep snow. Other times it would slap me in the face and I'd walk around with welts for a week."

Elliott also told of the incident that caused the demise of the Mall. It was at the point in chain-saw evolution when technology was finally delivering a decent one-man saw. One winter day my father and Elliott went to the Vermont Farm Show and saw a sleek new McCulloch. They examined it from its lightweight handle to the tip of its compact bar and chain. They especially marveled over a starter rope that emerged from a neat, yellow housing and recoiled with each pull. Elliott said he would have given his right arm for that saw but Dad said the Mall still had some life in it. Soon after that they were out logging in the bitter cold. Record deep snow made fighting with the Mall even worse and they had the old Allis Chalmers bull-dozer employed to plow paths and skid logs to a landing. One day Dad was backing the bulldozer up to hitch on a huge Hemlock log. It was almost chore time and the deep woods were getting dusky. Suddenly Elliott saw that the bulldozer was headed right toward the Mall.

"Watch out for the chain saw!" Elliott hollered at the top of his lungs. He heard my father's "Whaaaat?" and the clashing of metal on metal at the same time. When my father finally got the huge machine stopped, Elliott pointed to a twisted pile of steel in the snow. He said Dad got off the bulldozer, walked to the remains of the Mall, and leaned over it as in mourning. "He stayed like that for a minute," Elliott said. "When he turned toward me, he had a funny little grin on his face and he winked his eye." They went the next day and bought that new McCulloch.

Chapter 24

Vacations and the Grain Drain

THE SPRING PEEPERS have announced the end of sugarin' 2006 and I'm on to spring cleaning—that and catchin' my breath from a very busy sugar season. I love hearing those peepers. Sometimes I'll step out onto my lawn at night just to take in their song. They live in a swampy area down in the valley below my house. Beyond the peepers' domain lies a new lake, thanks to the beavers—or should I say "damn the beavers"? Beyond the new lake is a copse of fir trees that opens my view to the hills of Berlin and North-field. Nestled into those hills by day is the glitter of civilization, by night a thousand twinkling lights. The brightest lights are from the E. F. Knapp Airport and I especially love them because they bring thoughts and dreams of travel—my cheap trip.

There's something about the end of a busy season that makes me want to hit the road. I'm a farmer with too much to do but I do have the wan-derlust gene in my makeup. Right now I can't make up my mind. Betsy, my travel-hating angel of a wife, tells me to go. "You deserve a break," she says, but my mind gets creative: I think of a million idiots on the road, nights in strange places, and most especially, all that can go wrong in my absence—reminds me of the time Gerald Pease went on a trip and left me in charge of twenty cows, his "girls."

Before he left, Gerald went over a few basics. He reminded me that each of his two milking machines had a mind of its own and if I put the wrong machine on the wrong cow there'd be "hooves" to pay. I asked him if the cows always went in their own stanchion. His reply, last words to me before he left for two weeks, was curt and typical Gerald:

"If you grain 'em, by gory, they'll work with you."

It was early summer and the cows had just been turned out on green grass. That first morning as I drove up I could just make out their ghosts in the upper pasture through the early morning fog. "Good," I thought. "At least the critters are accounted for." I went into the barn and scanned the row of stanchions. Each cow's name was printed on a plaque above the stanchion, along with a hand-scribbled grain allotment. I drew a tub full from the grain chute that protruded from the ceiling and deposited it at each stanchion, secure that it was my single key to bovine relations. Next I went into the barnyard, unhooked an electric fence gate, and walked up the lane to a second gate. The cows ambled toward me like I had been their herdsman forever and allowed me to get behind them. They funneled into the lane and walked, some with bags dripping with milk, toward the barn. Once in the barn as Gerald had promised, each bovine entered a stanchion with total obedience; I knew it had nothing to do with intelligence, but a small amount of habit and piles of, you guessed it—grain.

As I assembled the two milking machines in Gerald's tidy milk house, I remembered our own family herd. I was not entirely green to the task of milking cows but sorely out of practice. My father had sold our herd ten years prior with the declaration that he would never milk another cow as long as he lived! "This won't be so bad," I thought, my third cup of coffee finally kicking in. I carried the milking machines out to the stable and approached the first cow, massaged her udder and slipped the machine on, one cup at a time. She swayed gently from side to side, but offered no resistance—I knew she was the right cow for the machine. The balance of the milking went with only a couple of minor skirmishes. I let the cows out, scraped down the barn, and tidied up the milk house before I returned for my daytime duties on the then cowless Morse Farm.

When I returned for night milking, I had an ominous feeling as my car climbed the ancient Culver Hill Road that leads to the Pease Farm. The sky was gloomy with a hint of rain in the air and when I turned left into Gerald's long driveway I noticed the entire herd of cows in the barnyard. "They must be anxious to see me again," I thought, knowing the fallacy of that notion. As I left my car and approached the herd I could see all was not well; they stood with vacant looks in their eyes, the bovine equivalent of sailors the day after. Their faces looked droopy and almost green. I walked through them, noticing the electric gate lying prostrate on the ground.

I shouted an earthy expletive to the Culver Hills—I had forgotten to close the gate when I left that morning! The barn door swayed unlatched, half open—another of my morning failures. I entered the stable and there stood my problem, like swift hoof to the groin—several tons of grain lay in a disturbed pile under the grain chute. Those creatures had worked the sliding door of the chute open and spent the entire day gorging themselves.

I glanced out the window at the post-orgy gathering: twenty unwilling, extremely stupified, and sick-to-their-stomach cows.

I knew I needed help and put in a mercy call to my father. When Dad answered, my first words were something like, "How much do you love me?" He arrived in an hour, suspecting, I'm sure, that his pledge to never milk another cow might be in jeopardy. We started the task by forming a two-man bucket brigade to return those tons of grain to the bin, one floor up. It took us five hours to somehow coax milk out of those cows, getting punched and violated in every imaginable way. When we finally finished, I thanked my father for saving me. His response said "you owe me big" in the form of a sideward glance.

Luckily all of the cows lived and I never did tell Gerald about the fiasco—best to spare that seed of worry and ruining his next vacation.

Last night I stepped outside my door again to hear the song of the peepers. The lights on yonder hillside were punctuated by the flashing airport strobes. They seemed to be saying hello to an approaching airplane that I knew would land, stay for a while, and take off, burning expensive gasoline on route to expensive places. It was a clear night, pre-bugs, and the Vermont beauty was staggering. My mind was made up—I would stay home, accept the springtime serenade and exercise my right to a cheap trip.

Chapter 25

Welcome Willows

OUR GOAT AND SHEEP recently busted out of their winter environs onto open range; there was no more putting it off...the fence had to be fixed. Fixin' fence is never a job that I enjoy but, what the heck, someone's gotta do it. Winter's always rough on fences, especially winters like this past one. Yesterday I found several of the aged boards splintered and prostrate and on the electric section the bottom wire lay ripped away from its broken insulators. I toggled it up, wishing I had all new materials, but that's the way with farming...you rarely can afford the materials to do a job right. My father was fixin' fence one time and he came up short of posts. He did what any resourceful farmer would have done...went to the nearest tree and cut out a few. The tree happened to be a willow, a species that grows fast, dies young, and is as prolific as a pair of rabbits. Dad said the next year when he attended to his fence duties, those improvised fence posts had sprouted roots and, by golly, had become trees!

I've spent my life farming this place and I've seen many crops go by the wayside because of poor drainage and soil that favors mavericks of the plant kingdom like witch grass, swale grass, and willow trees. I abandoned one of our crop fields years ago when water refused to follow the drainage ditch but instead found its way through the ledges and back into the field. Soon the field was so wet that mowing was impractical. From a distance, I watched its personality change from productive land to ragged vegetation to bushy trees. I didn't know what kind of trees they were but knew they were pests, like rats in the chicken house. Except for the town's interest every tax time, I declared it "no man's land" and left it alone.

Late last winter, a young man named Ryan Case approached me and said those trees over yonder were black willows; he seemed as excited as if he had found the mother lode right here on Morse Farm and asked for permission to take cuttings off them. "How much do I have to pay you to take 'em all?" I asked. Ryan laughed and explained that they would be used to stabilize the banks of portions of the Lamoille and Missisquoi rivers. The funding, he said, came from Governor Douglas's Clean and Clear Program for river management. I was excited to think there was something growing up in that quagmire that would help the environment and wasn't fazed when Ryan told me there was no money to pay for the "raw material."

Ryan and his willow crew showed up one day in early sugar season. They trudged over there on snowshoes and kept coming back day after day, rain or shine (my father used to say the best time in the world to work with propagating plants is in the pouring rain). Although I had no time to go over, from the distance I could see piles of brush accumulating. It felt good to have the additional spring activity happening on our farm. One day in late sugaring, my curiosity led me there for a quick inspection. The crew worked mostly with hand tools cutting seven-foot long whips from the trees and tying them into bundles of about six. Huge piles of those bundles lay waiting for transport. Ryan explained that each bundle would be placed horizontally in hand-dug trenches at the riverbank where about seventy-five percent would be left exposed to light and roots would set from the bottom twenty-five percent. He went on to say that willows only live to be fifteen or twenty years old. They serve to attract other riverbank species and also produce their own offspring in unique ways.

"The limbs are weak," he said, "and when live ones break off, they'll set roots and become new trees." I thought of my father's fence post trees long ago.

Ryan seemed relieved when I offered to transport the bundles out to the road with my tractor and trailer. My son Tommy hauled out a few loads and on the final day of cutting, I drove over for the last load. It was pouring rain that day and the crew looked forlorn in their yellow rain suits. They lugged the last of the bundles in from the bush and we hurriedly loaded my rig and headed back to the Morse Farm parking lot to Ryan's waiting truck.

Sugar season ended right after that, with lackluster results. That's three bad ones in a row but we maple sugarmakers get used to that; Mother Nature's in charge of both the outcome and the psychology...to make up for a lack of maple sweetness, she gave us an abundance of willows to serve the riverbanks for generations to come. She also improved my understanding that payback sometimes comes in good deeds done instead of dollars. We sugarmakers will just have to patiently wait. Soon enough, the next maple season'll take root and we'll try again.

Chapter 26

Wild Horses and Fried Chicken

I GOT A HUMOROUS response on my last column from a longtime friend, Mr. Mike Hutchinson. Mike was originally from Rochester, Vermont, and deserves inclusion for at least two reasons—he's a multi-generation Vermonter like me, and a fellow musician. In our younger years, we formed a band that played all around central Vermont. Needless to say, we had some "experiences of note" in that band, but first I'll relate Mike's comments on my last column:

"Your latest epistle brought back memories from Rochester when I was growing up and horses were still in use as the main, um, horsepower. Hey, we even had Central for our party- line phone connections!

"One old guy, a Polish native, had a horse-drawn wagon that he used to carry himself to a woodlot near my family's house and back to his house located some miles away. I was in grade school and returned to my house, after the bus let me off, by walking the eight-tenths -mile dirt road. Some marketing genius had developed a toy that was designed to be rotated and had rubber bands on a card, and a streamer and cord, so that when I whipped it around it would make a loud noise and the streamer would fly. Of course, I was fascinated and had to have it, even on my meager allowance.

"One day as I was walking home and whirling the toy, Mr. Bernal and his horse and wagon were going in the opposite direction. He saw me and yelled something at me, but I could not understand him. The horse saw the toy and was spooked, and took off in a gallop—fortunately following the road. Even now, I can see Mr. Bernal standing on that wagon alternately trying to the rein in the horse and yelling at him (the horse) and me in some strange language that neither of us could understand. I suspect my delicate ears were treated to words I'd never heard before and thus could not fully appreciate their translation."

Yes, Mike went on to make sounds of another kind, but not necessarily much less disruptive. The name of our group was The Congregation, patterned after Mike's church. We didn't get too many gigs, possibly because our name translated gospel "disharmony" to most folks—they wanted jazz. Once Mike, our piano player, marketer, and arranger extraordinaire, explained that we did play jazz, they slowly began to hire us. The trouble was, music was not the only thing we had in common—we were young, immature hellions!

One time we played at a local university where there were lavish amounts of food and drink for everyone in the house, including the band. Needless to say the bar was very popular at our first break, but I gravitated to the buffet table, magnetized by a mountain of fried chicken. There I mingled, for the purpose of absconding with huge amounts of the greasy stuff. What I didn't eat directly I smuggled away in napkins and pockets, right into the only container I had—my trombone case. The next night I was playing with another group at a high-security prison and somehow had forgotten events from the night before. We'd been told to bring only the bare necessities because we would be passing through multiple checkpoints—but I didn't plan on the dogs: As we approached the entrance to the prison, three highly trained security dogs descended on me like I was a smorgasbord. In the shake of a dog's tail, they wrested my trombone case to the ground, somehow prodded it open, and carried on like a Roman orgy—Oye! The fried chicken!

I watched, thinking of Barney Fife, as two red-faced officials leapt into the mêlée. They finally separated their thoroughly unprofessional dogs from scattered chicken remains, and then turned to me—they were not happy! As I remember the concert was well under way when I was finally allowed to join the rest of my group behind the bars. Those convicts sure did enjoy our strains of Glenn Miller and Count Basie. I've always hoped those guards eventually cooled down and saw the humor in that fried chicken caper.

Mike moved to Massachusetts years ago and the band immediately broke up. He has a fantastic Dixieland group down there called The Dixie Cats and still comes "home" occasionally with friendly e-mails. The other day I received a packet of old music from him, dating back to the old Congregation days. It included one of my arrangements of the 1970s pop song "Didn't We," re-done by Mike and his new music software.

"Thought you'd like to see a touched up version," Mike said, "without the beer stains and grease marks!"

As I scanned down the neat sheet of music, strangely foreign in my hand, I thought of the old days and how foreign they seem. We fear spooky drivers these days much more than spooking horses. And kids—well, kids're still hellions! I wish they'd content themselves with innocent toys and fried chicken capers but then kids are kids—they need to find their own way. The best we can hope for, in fact, is that everyone survives and will someday be able to sit back and say: "We finally grew up, didn't we."

Part Two
Faith Within

Chapter 27

A Springtime Bond

I RECENTLY RECEIVED a gracious critique of my book *Sweet Days & Beyond* from a Mr. Harmon "Rockie" Kelley, who received it as a Christmas present. Mr. Kelley has deep roots right in this neighborhood. He grew up just up the road from our place, went to the Morse School, and acquired his nickname, Rockie, as "the result of a blind date in the hills back of Plainfield" (he didn't elaborate any more on that subject). I grew up hearing stories about folks like Rockie Kelley and Beanie Bean, two East Montpelier tough guys who could have punched any challenger into the next county but didn't. Beanie spent a gentle life right here in East Montpelier as a finish carpenter and Rockie ended up in Rhode Island on another date; this one's lasted fifty-seven years so far. Rockie's comment on my book had to do with sugar-on-snow, or lack thereof. He intimated, in the kindest way, that not mentioning sugar-on-snow in a maple book is like not tappin' maple trees in the spring. You know, by gosh, I have to agree.

Let's just say sugar-on-snow is to Vermont maple sugaring what heavy cream is to milkin' cows—the end-all and be-all—the pièce de résistance. In fact the only thing good about my omission is that it prodded me to write a second book., And now that has happened, I'm going to borrow a few of Rockie Kelley's very well-constructed words:

"The sugarin'-off party was one of the social events of the neighborhood. Word would get around, most of it by the telephone party line, that Chester Anderson, our next door neighbor was going to sugar off that afternoon. Those invited were expected to bring a table fork and a large saucer."

He had my mouth watering already, yup—and then he went on: "Mr. Anderson had a smaller arch and a high-sided pan that held maybe sixty to seventy-five gallons into which he poured ten to fifteen gallons of syrup. It would boil up with big golden bubbles with him watching very closely. He had a wire with a two-inch loop on the end of it. He would dip the loop into the boiling syrup and blow through it and a string of bubbles six to twelve inches long would materialize from the loop. When the bubbles looked just right to him, out would come the fire on a big iron scoop shovel to be thrown out on the snow."

Once the fire was gone, Rockie explained, the guests held their snow-filled saucers out to Chester Anderson for a generous drizzling of boiled syrup. He also told of the dill pickles and the raised donuts (any Vermonter who holds a sugar party and leaves them out should be doused in frog-run maple syrup, feathered, and run out of state!). He said the stuff had the holding power of Gorilla Glue and those guests with false teeth either "pocketed them" or stood to become the afternoon's entertainment. He had me in stitches with his description of "a very large dog with a sweet tooth" and a whimpery case of temporary lockjaw! "At the time," he said, "it was very funny for the spectators."

Rockie's musings reminded me of one time we had a whole bus full of city folks eating sugar-on-snow on our open deck. As he suggested, sugar-on-snow is more than the sweetest treat this side of Saint Albans, Vermont, but it's also a social thing. Those city folks were having the greatest time picking blobs of amber ecstasy off the snow but they were not as savvy as the denture wearers at Chester Anderson's party—all of a sudden their patter rose to a group gasp and I looked up just in time to see a cemented set of dentures flying over the deck rail and down into the pasture below. It seems a woman had become flustered with the sticky situation and, in an attempt to be rid of the sweet resistance, had lost her teeth to boot. I'll al-ways remember that group of forty-five senior citizens, bent at the middle, scanning the Morse Farm countryside for those errant dentures!

The historical term for the event is "sugarin' off," and guys like Chester Anderson sold soft maple sugar in five-pound tins. Soft maple sugar is made by boiling maple syrup to a certain point where it'll stir and set-up into a light, coffee-colored sugar. Before it's stirred and poured, it's the per-fect consistency for sugar-on-snow. It was common back then to invite the neighbors in for the sugarin' off—business and pleasure mixed very nicely back in the good old days.

I called Rockie the other day. He has a soft, gentle voice and an obvious eye-twinkle for his wife, Nancy. They live in a huge old farmhouse on seven well-preserved acres in Westerly, Rhode Island. He's eighty-five now, said he didn't know if he'd ever come back to Vermont again, but was proud that two of his five grown children have migrated back as long-time residents. In fact those guys, Pete and Dick, come up to our place once in a while when we're serving sugar-on-snow. I'm sure they don't like it quite like Rockie did but they've gotta come—they inherited Rockie's Vermont genes, thick and well glued, like sugar-on-snow.

I'd like to tell you how you can make sugar-on-snow on a small scale in your kitchen, wherever you live: Put one-third cup of Fancy or Grade A Medium Amber maple syrup into a microwavable bowl and add a dab of butter (so that it doesn't spatter all over your microwave). Microwave on high for three minutes. Make some damp snow from ice cubes with your food processor or just go outside and get a bowl full (especially if you live in New York City or Boston). Pour the maple sugar you have microwaved onto the snow. Pick it up in taffy-form with a fork. Don't eat the snow and don't forget the pickles!!!

May your day be sweet and your teeth stay put.

Chapter 28

A Bite Outa Burr

'TIS THE SEASON OF PEACE and goodwill to all men. Being a person of faith, I believe that there is much more wiggle room in human relationships around the world than the news would have us believe. Because of this farm, I've been pretty much welded to Central Vermont which limits my knowledge of the rest of the world. I have, however, had the good fortune of traveling to Russia a couple times in the last ten years and can attest to the universal love I found from the countrymen and women of that ancient and wonderful place. Those folks (the countrymen, not the leaders) have locked the last remnants of the Cold War solidly in a closet and replaced it with a huge red carpet. However, there is another segment of the Russian populace that hasn't heard that the wall came down: the animals. It is by the claws and teeth of Russian animals that I alternately have had the crap beat out of me and my life threatened during those two trips.

We were out at our Russian family's country dacha on our first visit. They had killed a sheep the day before to prepare a shish kabob for us, their special visitors. It was a perfect July evening in the flat farm country surrounding Kirov and we—Betsy, our two sons and I—met with our huge extended Russian family. The purpose of my family's trip was to celebrate the life of Alex, our Russian exchange student, our son and brother, who had died shortly after he returned to Russia from his year in our Vermont home.

His family, still in grief, was ecstatic to have us visit; their red carpet included not only the gathering at the dacha but concerts, tours, gift-giving and laughter in Kirov, a central Russian city of 500,000. It also included vodka, which I had been told by seasoned Russian visitors was not mandatory; being non-seasoned and slightly stupid, I drank it anyway. We partied into the night; being so far north, the sky was strangely light at 10 p.m. On one of my trips to the one-holer, which stood at the back end of a series of barns and connecting buildings, I chose an alternate route through the hen house. I had no sooner closed the gate behind me when all hell broke loose; I believe it was a single rooster that was upon me, although the vodka was presenting things in twos and threes by that time. A vicious combination of claws and beak flailed unmercifully, leaving no doubt that it would not stop until I was dead. I groped for the hasp on the hen house door and after considerable fumbling with the hand that wasn't shielding my eyes and other vulnerable body parts, I opened it, fell through, and slammed it on some part of the then-squawking killer. The episode was not mentioned when I returned to the party, and the vodka, my wife later said, led me toward other equally foolish subjects. To this day, however, I bear scars on both shins as proof of that vicious attack!

On our next trip to Russia, we were visiting our friends, Vladimir and Luda, in the tiny village of Rushkiel. Vladimir had been manager of Rushkiel's huge collective farm pre-Perestroika. The couple, both veterinarians by trade, lived in a small house at the edge of the farm's flat fields. On that trip I had finally learned to say "nyet" to the vodka and found myself doing healthier things like strolling out back to get a closer look at the fields. All of a sudden, quicker than you could say Mikhail Gorbachev, a snarling beast appeared from nowhere; his intentions left no need for translation. Instinctively, I lunged away from my attacker, doing a perfect somersault out onto the Russian plowed ground. Fortunately, the German shepherd reached the end of his substantial chain just as I began my lunge.

Unfortunately, he tore a chunk out of both my jeans and my left buttock before being finally restrained. My hosts rushed to calm the dog, help me up and guide me into the house. I knew I would be OK but could not discourage the Russians from immediate first aid. One woman demanded my pants and from the embarrassing position that Vladimir coaxed me into, I could see her already sewing on the tear. Vladimir examined my wound and Luda appeared with a potion she had been preparing. The vets insisted I drink it, which I did with no complaint. I sit here six years and a couple buttocks scars later, grateful for the huge Russian red carpet and their potion as well.

Yes, I believe there's more room for peace than war among the world's people. As for relations with the world's animals, I suggest less vodka and more common sense. We've all gotta live here, so let's make that red carpet even bigger in 2008. Happy New Year.

Chapter 29

The Call of Nature

A COUPLE MONTHS AGO I wrote on the subject of getting "caught short" on an airplane. I'm sorry to overwork the subject but stories of peeing can be funny; I hope you'll allow me to get it all out of my system, so to speak. Autumn's on the wane but we still have a few buses coming to our place. Even though our slide show is less than ideal in our chilly, late autumn sugarhouse, we still invite bus folks in. This morning we had a group that had ridden the whole bumpy way from New Hampshire with coffee-filled bladders. A few had distressed looks on their faces and I immediately directed them to the loo (they were English). The majority, however, followed me into the sugarhouse, saying they could "hold it" for my twelve-minute presentation on maple sugaring. I had a strange feeling about the wisdom of the wait and as they settled into the cold seats, my feeling grew even stronger. Suddenly I realized we faced a potential "perfect storm" of bladder limits...the ride, the coffee, the cold seats, and the laughter that would soon begin. Yes, over the years, my presentation has accumulated a few funny lines with proper delivery and the same lines that make the average person chuckle were hilarious to these folks. One guy, in particular, had a loud, goofy laugh which ignited the whole group into a roof-raisin' frenzy. All of sudden, there was enough energy in that old sugarhouse to boil a whole year's worth of maple syrup...I began to wonder if they had drunk more than just coffee over there in New Hampshire!

Just before the show ended, I noticed an added dynamic—part of my crowd was standing up performing strange little stooped dances and the knees of those seated swayed back and forth, speaking the unmistakable language of full bladders. The second my presentation was over, the crowd rushed the door and charged, guided by some sort of internal GPS, toward the restrooms in the next building. I remember the man with the goofy laugh shouting, "I ALMOST FELL OFF ME BLOODY CHAIR WITH YER BLINKIN' HUMOR AND ME FLOATIN' EYEBALLS...

WHERE'S THE BLOODY LOO?" They were still laughing as they boarded their bus an hour later; tears dripped from their eyeballs but their fronts were dry...guess they "skipped to the loo" on time!

My wife, Betsy, tells another story related to the subject of tourists and answering nature's call. Our house sits just 300 feet from our sugarhouse and store and folks walk close to it on our Maple Trail. One fall day when our place had several big tour buses there at the same time, Betsy returned from taking her wheelchair-bound mother for a long ride. Mother needed to use the facilities PDQ, so Betsy wheeled her right into our only bathroom. Betsy, in turn, retreated to the back entrance to use the great outdoors. Our back entrance faces only wilderness so she squatted down underneath her favorite lilac bush, not having all the time in the world. Suddenly she sensed another presence. She looked up and there, standing thirty feet away, was a family of Asian folk who had strayed from the Maple Trail. She said they stood, open-mouthed at the spectacle before them.

A situation like that would have made most people panic and get all red in the face but my Betsy's not most people. She just finished what she was doing, stood up, and, beckoning toward the idling tour buses, shouted in her best Ma Kettle voice: "Ya...the old man says if those tour buses keep comin', he's goin' ta get us some indoor plummin'." The family smiled nervously, waved, and walked away.

Betsy and I both grew up in Vermont in the '50s. Back then just about everything could be solved out back of the barn or behind a tree. These days agri-tourism has altered our styles just a bit, but we're not complaining. We learned to laugh at ourselves and with others back there on the farm. We also learned that nature keeps a callin', times change, and you gotta do what you gotta do.

Chapter 30

Rivers of Change

WHEN I GO TRAVELING, I try to seek out as many friendly folk as possible. I also keep my ears open for interesting stories about the places I go. My last two winter trips have, for some reason, brought stories about rivers and the strange things they sometimes do. Last year I went to western Tennessee and visited my friend Earl Hinkel. Earl was a gracious host and showed me, among many other things, Reelfoot Lake. Reelfoot is a 15,000-acre shallow lake that was instantly born back in the early 1800s when an earthquake caused the Mississippi River to flow backward. This year brought me to Kansas City and my brother-in-law and his wife, Chuck and Anne Parker. They really rolled out the "Show Me" red carpet but I was especially interested in a story they told about the Missouri River. Near Kansas City, it seems, a couple of local families found a nineteenth- century steamboat buried forty feet deep in the middle of a corn field...in that 100 years the mighty Missouri had moved its course one-half mile away from where the boat had sunk!

The story piqued my interest so much that they took me to the Steamboat Arabia Museum which proved to be both very enlightening and probably the friendliest place east of the Missouri. We drove into an empty parking lot in the wintry center of Kansas City, parked, and entered the modern, glassed-faced facade. Although we were the only tourists there at that time, the two young women who greeted us were friendly and outgoing. One introduced herself as our guide and began our tour by explaining the quirks of the Missouri River, its importance to the development of the West, and that it was often hostile to the steamboats that plied its waters.

We learned that the *Arabia*, a 171-foot boat built in Brownsville, PA, was punctured by a sunken tree while churning up the Missouri and sank in 1856. All 130 people aboard were saved but its entire cargo, which included 400 barrels of the finest Kentucky whiskey, sank to the bottom. It remained in its burial site for over 100 years while the Missouri moved elsewhere until two local guys, Bob Hawley and Jerry Mackey, finally located it in 1988. The hole they dug ended up as big as a football field before the Arabia and its precious bounty could be salvaged, piece by piece. All this was done on a shoestring budget with a raw determination that none of the artifacts would ever be sold but preserved forever in a museum...and what a wonderful museum it became!

We walked past neat displays that showed off an amazing assortment of the *Arabia*'s cargo: jars of pickles, shoes, hats, clothing, beads, buttons, old square nails, guns, tools, tens of thousands of articles that all had to be preserved in just the right way. A woman in the museum's lab explained the different processes required for preserving wood, leather, and iron. At the time, she was working on a huge iron board saw that had to be all gone over with a dental pick to remove the corrosion! The highlight of our tour was when Bob Hawley himself approached and graciously answered questions from our inquisitive group of three. By that time we had seen the video that told the whole fascinating story portraying the entire Hawley family and their passion for the project...to us Bob Hawley was a celebrity and we were so proud that he would want to talk to us.

It has been a few weeks since my return to Vermont and the grind of everyday life. Yesterday I went down by the brook that intersects our farm. I don't suppose our brook will ever create a whole lake or sink a steamboat but it always does its own weird thing every year about now. Almost pompously, it swells with spring runoff shouting an introduction to our own natural phenomenon, maple sugarin'. Sugarin's about running water—sap water. It's on a smaller scale than the great rivers of our country but holds an allure all its own. Sugarin's why many tourists come to Vermont and every maple family stands ready to tell their story with friendliness and passion, just like our counterparts to the west.

Chapter 31

The Gift of Horses

WE RECENTLY EMPLOYED Meryl and Skip Buck and their two Oberlander horses, Sarah and Gallo, for an open house at Morse Farm. I had heard about the Bucks from Brookfield, Vermont, and knew they gave wagon rides on occasion. I called Merle and explained that we needed the perfect team, screening her much like a parent screens a potential childcare provider. "I've been drivin' horses since I was a small girl," Merle said, "and Skip comes along to keep law and order." She spoke with an honest, Vermont voice and I quickly understood that we were not talking "beasts of burden," but an extended family—a business partnership. She said that Sarah and Gallo are alumni of the Anheuser Busch organization and ended up with the Bucks through a rigid placement process. "They're wonderful horses and work together well with Skip and me," she said. Her only minor disclaimer was that Sarah had recently had a bout of bursitis and was in a little pain. Merle assured me, however, that she would be fine and the exercise would do her good.

Shortly before the rides were to begin, a white truck pulling a horse trailer pulled into our yard. The trailer rocked on its springs and an occasional *bang* emitted from inside. Skip and Meryl, a happy-looking, middle-aged couple, got out of the truck and introduced themselves. "Those rascals are always excited to begin workin'," Skip joked to the obligatory onlookers. He hurried to the back of the trailer, unlatched the doors and when he led the first horse down the ramp, the onlookers drew a collective gasp. The animal before us was stunning and noble—probably the most beautiful horse any of us had ever seen. Its coffee-vanilla mane hung down to highlight its huge sorrel body. It also looked kind and intelligent.

Meryl brought out the second horse, which was equally stunning, and Skip began harnessing them. When he was done, he led them close to the wagon that had been brought to Morse Farm on an earlier trip. He coaxed them backward to straddle the wagon pole and then allowed them to relax.

As the onlookers gathered closer to ask questions and take turns at patting the friendly faces, Sarah seemed a bit ill at ease. Meryl showed concern, like a mother with a sick child. "Sarah, you've got to settle down. I don't know what's got in to you!" she chided. Sarah continued to misbehave and, all of a sudden, Meryl uttered, "That's enough!" She grabbed Sarah's halter and strode off to the edge of the parking lot. I heard a round-eyed little girl mutter to her dad, "Time out for horses." When they returned, Sarah appeared contrite and ready to work with Gallo.

I stood and watched as the first group headed out across our pasture. Meryl sat high up at the reins and Skip stood at the back of a happy crowd, no doubt offering tidbits of Vermont wisdom. As I watched, it occurred to me that I had previously downplayed the difficulties of horse travel. Unlike motorized vehicles, horses are intelligent beings with unique personalities. Every task first requires the heavy and specialized job of harnessing, and then psychology—chemistry between humans and horses. Several times throughout the day, the horses simply stopped for rests, voicing their upper hand to the humans. Sarah and Gallo somehow communicated to each other about when it was time to rest and when it was time to resume. It was obvious from the distance that the two teams of Bucks were perfect together.

This chemistry is not guaranteed and I recall stories told by my grandfather of the horrors that arose when drivers and horses clashed. One particular story is more about the driver than the horse, but very entertaining—motor vehicles have brought both a drought of horse travel and of the folklore that goes with it.

Grandpa Morse told of a man from Hardwick who was traveling south, toward Montpelier, down through Woodbury Gulf. He came across another man he recognized as, in the vernacular of the day, a simpleton. The simpleton was in the middle of the road beating his horse with a leather strap. The Hardwick man stopped his team and approached. "See here," he said. "You must stop beating that creature of God—don't you know that Christ died for your sins?" To that, the guy stopped, peered up at the man from Hardwick and said, "Chroyst doyd? —musta happened when Dad and I was down to Chelsea!"

I learned a lot from the teams Buck that day and will certainly employ them again and again. Life has gotten much easier with modern travel but ease is not always the best medicine. We've surely sacrificed common sense and a certain camaraderie in the transition. It was obvious in the shouts of joy I heard that day as the horses went like the wind down the other side of grades they had just labored to go up. It's those "peaks and valleys" of travel that have been streamlined and flattened out that we miss—a certain crispness to life and closeness to God—well, except, maybe, for that day up in Woodbury Gulf.

Dr. Laqueur arrives at his new summer home.
Harry Morse and his tractor in the background.

Back in my Glenwood days.

My high school graduation photo.

Robby, me and Tommy...I played with them but Betsy made them practice!

Peering into a sap bucket.

Greeting more tourists at the Morse Farm Sugarhouse.

Chuck Parker and me in Kansas City in winter of 2008...
couldn't find Genesee so we toasted with Margaritas.

The reason I went to LA was to learn the art of popping kettle corn.

Doin' my impression of a woodchuck!

Laurina Holt and Fern, good friends of Morse Farm, highlight Betsy's flowers.

Christmas tree shoppers at the Morse Farm.

Playing New Year's Eve 2007 at Mount Washington Hotel with
Swing North Big Band.

A Curious Jersey.

My wonderful parents, Harry and Dot Morse.

Uncle Ira Morse.

My grandpa Sydney's wonderland of barns.

My parents and my mother's dad, Senator Aiken.

Four page boy buddies visit Washington. Left to right: me, Greg Raymond, Vice President Lyndon Johnson, Jimmy Kennedy, Byron Hathorne, my grandfather, Senator Aiken.

Hamming it up with my pretty Russian friend, Marina.

The dreaded Russian rooster pen.

Tommy "trading fours" with Lester Bowie.

Me on Palmer Beach in Alburg, Vermont.

Betsy and our Russian boy's mother, Tanya, in Nizhny Novgorod.

Russian Shish Kabob.

Alex's parents with Robby and Tommy Morse, their American boys.

Betsy and Alex...Our Russian Boy.

Rob Morse plays with Trey Anastasio of the band, Phish

Miriam Bernardo, gardener supreme

Family portrait: Betsy, Tommy, Robby, Burr

My mother and father, Dot and Harry Morse, in the world's first RV.

2002 Northwest Folklife Festival in Seattle, Washington.

Photo by Larry Perry

Father and son

Neighbor Carroll Badger's sugarhouse with Oliver Cletrac, work horse of the time, in foreground.

Wagon ride at Morse Farm.

Golden Times in Vermont
PHOTOGRAPHS BY DAVID AIKEN

THE WHITE HOUSE

WASHINGTON

April 27, 1960

Dear Mr. and Mrs. Morse:

A group of high school students from Montpelier
left with Senator Prouty, who delivered it to me,
a gallon of the justly famous Vermont maple
syrup. I understand you were good enough to
give the syrup to the group, and this note brings
to you my warm and personal thanks for your
kindness.

With best wishes,

Sincerely,

Dwight Eisenhower

Mr. and Mrs. Sydney Morse
Montpelier
Vermont

J. W. FULBRIGHT, ARK., CHAIRMAN

HN SPARKMAN, ALA.   GEORGE D. AIKEN, VT.
KE MANSFIELD, MONT.   KARL E. MUNDT, S. DAK.
BERT GORE, TENN.   CLIFFORD P. CASE, N.J.
ANK CHURCH, IDAHO   JOHN SHERMAN COOPER, KY.
UART SYMINGTON, MO.   JOHN J. WILLIAMS, DEL.
OMAS J. DODD, CONN.   JACOB K. JAVITS, N.Y.
AIBORNE PELL, R.I.
LE W. MC GEE, WYO.

         CARL MARCY, CHIEF OF STAFF
         ARTHUR M. KUHL, CHIEF CLERK

United States Senate

COMMITTEE ON FOREIGN RELATIONS
WASHINGTON, D.C. 20510

May 4, 1970

Mr. Harry Morse, Jr.
County Road
Montpelier, Vermont   05602

Dear Burr:

Don't get too upset over the current happenings. The history of the United States is for the most part one of one crisis right after another. During the eight years Eisenhower was President, we were comparatively free of major troubles but that was the exception rather than the rule.

I think President Nixon made a bad mistake, although there is one chance in a hundred that his new strategy may work. However, he will have a great deal of trouble both in this country and other countries in making people believe him from now on. I think he was on the right course up till last week and would have had all our troops out of Viet Nam within the next two or three years.

I am getting several hundred telegrams and letters every day. They are running about eight to one in opposition to the President's position. The people who got us into this mess in the first place are apparently very happy now since he has taken much of the blame off of them.

Keep up your courage. This crisis will be over someday and then we will have another. Maybe the next one will be about money -- who knows.

Sincerely yours,

GEORGE D. AIKEN

GDA:mam

Chapter 32

Heaven for Different Folks

How many times have we all heard the old adage, stop and smell the roses? It sure was popular in my family, only it had a lot more to do with the roses than the attitude. You see, I come from a family of flower lovers. My parents' idea of Nirvana was to head off to a greenhouse, walk up and down the aisles bursting with "oohs and aahs," and cradling blossoms like newborn babies. Places like Longwood Gardens and the Boston Flower Show were heaven on a human scale to them. They've now gone on to the real heaven and I'm absolutely sure it offers flowers galore.

They were so in love with the floral world that they assumed it would automatically pass on to their progeny and I for one, as one-quarter of that progeny, have always felt like a black sheep; flowers are OK from a distance but I'm quite ignorant about them, never "ooh and aah," and never, EVER cradle them like babies! This all came back to me the other day when I walked past my wife mixing manure and other earthy ingredients for the flower boxes and beds down at our store. I thought of my parents doing the same thing year after year and ending up with solid banks of brilliance and flower-punctuated pathways. Frankly I always had more appreciation for the manure; now there's something that has a purpose—makes a real difference. Manure is beautiful!

Betsy, my better half, makes up for my deficit. She's happiest when she's doing something with plants and I suspect my parents watch, pleased, from their celestial perch while looking askance at me, hoping I'll grow up sometime and smell the roses. My siblings all got the flower gene, especially my sister Susie. Her house overlooks purple, majestic mountains, amber waves of grain, and spacious skies but she's still not satisfied until she plants ninety-nine percent of God's floral offerings to smile upon that view. Brother Elliott knows the Latin names of everything from stinkin' benjamin to dutchman's britches and brother Sherwood takes lots of folks to a secret lady slipper swamp, only if they swear on a stack of *Better Homes and Gardens* that they'll never tell where they went. My cousin, David Aiken, takes the most avid/verging on whacko award, however, for flower chasing. He routinely drives all over the East Coast, photographing blossoms and the bees and hummingbirds that make love to them. He has got some great pictures but, by God, he'll keep trying until he finds the botanical equivalent of Romeo and Juliet or hell freezes over.

Suspecting at an early age that I was different, I made a conscious decision to go toward music, figuring if I couldn't keep it all in the family I could at least keep it all on the right side of the brain. One day the Ellis Music Company guy came to my fourth-grade class and, in the mad rush of unbuckling cases and parceling out, I suppose, what needed to be sold that day, I ended up with a trombone. Although I've tried every trick in the method book to quit since then, destiny has led this self-conscious admirer of cow manure to be a life-long trombone player. I've spent that tenure seeking out God's most beautiful piece of music, one that would rival a quadruple row of foxgloves, lightly sprinkled with pink and white peonies.

Finally, after fifty years of the good search, I found it last week while playing a concert with the Vermont Philharmonic Orchestra. Weekly rehearsals had hinted that "Nimrod," from Sir Edward Elgar's "Enigma" Variations might be a possible candidate but, as rehearsals go, flaws persisted like weeds in a flowerbed. On concert night, however, Lou Kosma, bassist for the Metropolitan Opera and our intrepid director, dredged near-perfection from the sixty-odd Vermont musicians and one botanically challenged trombone player. I'll never forget the free-flying emotions that filled the hall that night as we caressed every measure of "Nimrod." After it was over, I looked out at the ornate confines of the Barre Opera House and saw, I swear, the beaming faces of Harry and Dot Morse clapping with the best of 'em. "It's OK now, Burr," they seemed to say. "We believe in your kind of beauty."

Chapter 33

Holy Sugarin'

I BECAME SIXTY YEARS OLD today...yup, you've heard it before but I'll say it one more time: Where did the time go? Fifty-five years ago on this day, I would have been lookin' up at my father handling the dippers and hydrometers of sugarhouse boiling but today, I was doing the handling myself. It was also, besides my birthday, our first real day of boiling—the day to get all the bugs out, so to speak. The good news is that I feel more like the five-year-old than the sixty-year-old. The bad news (not that there's ever really any bad news in sugarin') is that on that first day of boiling, I get a little bit cranky. These days we have lots of people wandering into our sugarhouse and depending on how bad those "bugs" are, I can look like a damned fool or a raving maniac.

Early in the day, as I was preparing the evaporator for duty, I heard a tap, tap, tap up by the road. I climbed the ladder to a platform that holds one of the sap tanks and offers a view to the County Road. From there, I heard a door slam and saw a white car taking off up the road. I would have suspected foul play had I not recognized the car as belonging to my friend, Rich Davidian. Rich's wife, Shawn, is one of these angels who keeps track of birthdays so I knew Rich's mission had something to do with my special day. I had no sooner started boiling when horns began honking outside the sugarhouse; this area of East Montpelier, Vermont, sounded like the corner of Broadway and 42nd Street for the rest of the day—Rich had put out a sign up that said: "Honk to say Happy 60th Birthday to Burr"!

I won't say there wasn't considerable stress on that first day of boiling but the stress didn't come in the form of breakdowns; the equipment worked sweetly, like the springtime elixir that it prepared. The steam that rises when making that elixir, in turn, brought hordes of folks with noses raised in appreciation of the aroma and queries needing to be answered about this unique process. My major stress was over the shortage of sap and fears that I could lose track and ruin the evaporator by running it dry.

One of our mid-morning guests was my great friend from over in North-field, Mr. Bill Pemberton. Bill, judging by remnants of an accent foreign to Vermont, originated down where honking horns rule the day—Long Island. He came to Vermont as a young man to play Norwich University football and big band music. Somewhere in the process, he married a real "Vermontah," and took on the maple gene by osmosis. Bill taps fifteen trees over in Northfield and has sugared religiously for about fifty years. He threatened to give it up last year due to age but I knew he couldn't. He came in the sugarhouse led by a handmade maple cane and congratulated me for the great sap run we were having.

"Great sap run, the hell!" I said. "Sap's just barely trickling today...now don't be tellin' me it's runnin' like mad just ten miles away in Northfield."

"By God it is...tickin' it right off," he replied in that accent that oddly belies a Vermont maple sugarmaker. I knew from the look on his face that he was not lying and began to fret about how weather could be so different in two towns just ten miles apart. Then, with a twinkle in his eye, he reminded me his trees are just behind Northfield's Catholic Church. "When I want somethin' good to happen wit' those maple trees, I just look up at that steeple and....voila!" Bill and I had a good laugh and I was still chuckling when he left, thinking, "He really has been sugarin' 'religiously'"!

In the same vein, I was talking to Gerianne Smart, chief marketer for *Vermont Life* magazine yesterday. She asked me how the maple season was going. I told her that the weather remained a little too cold for sap to run well and that we sugarmakers were a bit frustrated to be missing peak sugarin' days over a few degrees of warmth. When I suggested to Gerianne that she "ask God" if she wanted any better explanation than that, her reply was instant and witty like only a marketer extraordinaire could come up with: "Oh God's busy with Easter right now, Burr...he'll get to the weather in all good time!"

Yes, we've begun sugarin' and it's been a different sort of year so far. My "angel" friend, Shawn, arranged a honkin' good first day of boiling. I was visited by the most "religious" sugarmaker of them all, and a top marketer assured me that gratification has its priorities even at the highest levels. I sit here finishing up this column knowing the day outside is still too cold for a sap run. That old adage, if you don't like what's happening with Vermont weather, just wait a few minutes, comes to mind. I'm patiently waiting for a rise of a few degrees and the sweetness that I know will come...Thank God.

Chapter 34

Journey to the Nord

I'VE ALWAYS HAD AN attitude about our neighbors north of the 45th parallel. Even though my car can take me there in a mere sixty minutes, the language is different and entrance is gained only through a gate with armed guards—it's a foreign country.

The other day my brother Elliott asked me to accompany him and his Civil War Roundtable group across the border to visit the Abenaki Museum at Odanak. When I demurred, he said I could sleep on it and give him the answer the next day. That night when I checked the atlas to locate Odanak, the straight edge that physically separates Vermont from Quebec jumped out at me. "Makes as much sense as a flat-top haircut on a round-faced boy," I thought.

Perhaps my most radical bias, however, is over something that should be peaceful—maple syrup. Quebec is a huge maple region and its competition with Vermont has not always been, shall we say, sweet. In spite of my reservations, I decided to make the trip. We met members of the Roundtable early in the morning at a shopping center parking lot in Derby Line. In the carpool shuffle, Elliott and I welcomed Ed Bearss, a nationally known historian on American wars, as our passenger.

We proceeded, caravan style, to the Canadian Customs Station at Rock Island, Quebec. I was surprised there was no waiting line but nevertheless was on edge, envisioning my Nissan Altima being ripped to pieces by sharp knives and pry bars. A female Customs agent came to the passenger window, asked where we were going, and requested our identification cards. "What are you taking into Canada?" she also asked. Inwardly I screamed "bad attitude, prejudice and the ability to make better maple syrup." Outwardly I said, "Nothing but our personal items." After a short time, she handed back our IDs, waved us on, and wished us a good day. "That's all," I thought, feeling like a prisoner suddenly on the outside.

As we headed north, Ed Bearss entertained us with tales of the massacre by Rogers' Rangers at Odanak, back in 1759. It seems Rogers' Rangers traveled up from Crown Point to the settlement of Saint-Francis (the very sight of the present-day Abenaki Museum) and massacred the Indians, starting with women and children. Ed's portrayal of the English, my ancestors, strangely tempered my mood as the Quebec countryside passed by and the conversation continued. After 160 kilometers our final road, Route 143 "Nord," brought us to a bridge over the Saint Francis River and into the parking lot of the Abenaki Museum. Our caravan had stayed intact and our leader, Tony O'Connor, led us into the museum's lobby. We were introduced to Rodrigo, who would be our guide. Rodrigo started the tour at a wall map that showed the Abenaki Nation, a huge area that included present-day New England, right up to the St. Lawrence River. My eyes beheld not only an Indian nation, but a mammoth maple region, undivided and unspoiled by competition.

Rodrigo continued on to show us a rebuilt version of the church that was burnt during the massacre. It had a wonderful, peaceful feel with wood-carved statues and wood-relief carvings lining the walls, obviously reflecting Abenaki craftsmanship. He told us details of the massacre and answered our many questions. The tour went on through the museum, which was spotlessly clean and very well done. The most striking section was a rooftop panorama of the Saint Francis River with special viewfinders that showed the river scene the way it was in 1759, complete with canoes full of approaching Rangers.

The hit of the day, however, was at noon. We had been told that a meal would be prepared for our group, but were especially honored to have members of the present-day Abenaki nation sit down with us. The pièce de résistance, however, came when Abenaki women served a traditional meal including corn bread, venison steak, and fiddlehead ferns! We had a wonderful dinner hour with those peaceful folks, talking one-on-one about the history that had brought us there that day.

Our tour ended soon after dinner with a return to the lobby. We left our hosts with the usual handshaking and goodbyes, but there were no words or gestures for the true magnitude of our appreciation. We had passed a modern-day peace pipe in a different country, but the feeling was more like there were no borders. Back in our cars, we talked about the highlights of our adventure. The same 160 kilometers delivered us south to the reality of a gate with armed guards. We drove up to the U.S. Customs and were asked, again, for our IDs and where we had been. When the stern, uniformed man asked what we were bringing into the U.S., I said, "Just memories of a great day." I said nothing about all the "baggage" I had left on the shore of the Saint Francis River.

Chapter 35

Night Owl

OK, I'LL ADMIT TO BEING a poor sleeper but that's as far as I'll go—I'm not crazy! It's just that...well...the rest of this story sounds a little bizarre. Bizarre or not, here it is.

Sometimes when I'm awake in the middle of the night, especially on the nights when the moon offers a look to the valley below, I see an owl sitting up in the white birch tree out in our backyard. The tree is just feet from my bed, a shoe's throw away for an undesirable creature but not an owl...I'm always proud to have an owl sit and stare at me. A few nights ago while held in the same old nocturnal limbo, I noticed the owl was back. This time I stepped out through my sliding glass door to get a closer look. The night was surreal, painted by a whitish meadow frost against the moon-lit sky. Surprisingly, Mr. Owl, instead of swooping away, swiveled his big owl head right in my direction. We momentarily locked eyes and then something happened that just about made me jump outa my BVDs, which was all I had on at the time; a strange, cooing voice came directly from the tree: "Hears lookin' at youooowhooooooo."

"What?" I said.

The owl stared intensely. His only movement was to shift from one foot to the other.

"Excuse me," I said, feeling foolish, "but did you talk?"

He continued to stare, blinking occasionally. It was when my own eyes, giving in to human embarrassment, turned toward the distant valley, that the cooing voice returned.

"Got two chances...I either don't or I dooooowhoooooo."

"Well then you dooooowhooooo," I exclaimed, mimicking his inflection. "That's amazing! I've seen you here many nights..."

The owl interrupted. "Please excuuuwhoooose...I'll be right back." He lifted off and flew, gracefully, down toward my basement door. I heard a flapping sound, and then he was back on the limb carrying a small, squirming mass in his claws. He spoke again, this time longer and more intimately.

"Don't mean to be ruuuuuwhooooode, but it's my mealtime. I come here cause you got a rodent problem. This rascal was just about to set up housekeeping in your basement and I love a good fat mouse...you know, one hand washes twooooowhoooooooo."

He popped the mass into his mouth and proceeded to make a satisfied crunching sound. "Love the crunch of a young cranium...probably the difference, to you, between Jif crunchy and Jif smoowhooooth," he said, surprising me with his knowledge of my own taste in peanut butter.

"Boy, you are smart, just like they say, but I really question the wisdom of eating a mouse," I said, being a bit of a wise guy.

Quick as the blink of an eye, he placed remnants of the mass back down at his feet and puffed his body up to twice its size. "I suppose you'd have me eat pepperoni laced with sodium nitrite and red dye number twoooowhooooo!" he shouted, obviously rankled. Then, just as quickly, he deflated back to normal size and resumed eating.

"Touché," I said, deciding to change the subject. "By the way, I'd like to ask your opinion about something. We humans are having a tremendous argument about this global warming business. Some think we're causing it with things we do, like flying here and there in airplanes. Others say it's just nature acting out like nature does. What do you think?" He grabbed the mass with his claws, stretched it out until it broke with a snap and continued eating the broken-off piece.

"Well...there's wisdom in them wings but you gotta watch what you power 'em with." He paused to spit out a beady eyeball " ...and remember, in the end nature ruuuuwhooooles the roooowhoooost."

"Wow," I said. "You're not making it easy...I gotta think about that one."

"Thinkin's gooooowhoood," he replied, doing nothing to ease my confusion. "Now if you don't mind, daybreak's coming and I gotta get to bed. I live in a spruuuuuuwhooose tree down by the Winooooowhoooski and it's a ways to go."

With that he moved to a tree nearby where I swear I heard him say: "Not a bad stop at all...netted a fat young mouse and made a damn fooooowhoool think." Just before he left for good, there was an unmistakable "hahahawwhowhowhoooooo!"

Chapter 36

It's Not About the Tree

THE WORDS CAME OUT soft and under his breath, like we were dealing in something illegal: "I'd just as soon have a four footer — one that fits nicely into a corner and doesn't fight you all the way — keep that under your hat."

"My lips are sealed," I whispered.

He and the missus had just made their annual rounds of our Christmas tree lot, tape measure in hand, examining the larger trees. They finally settled on the ten- foot beauty, a step down from their usual fourteen-footer. They've been coming to our place for years; she loves big, fluffy Christmas trees and he's always there with equal-size support. I've watched their love story unfold for many of the thirty-six years I've been a Christmas tree peddler, but, alas, they're crowding old age now and, in his words, "gotta size down."

Over the course of that thirty-six years, I've seen a lot of Christmas tree psychology— the humorous, the touching and the downright prickly. I must admit that I'm capable of "the prickly" but have kept it under my hat all these years. You see, Christmas trees have grown in America, like cars and couches, from the spindly ones that nature offers to perfectly manicured farm trees. We seed 'em, weed 'em, sheer 'em, and feed 'em—and they get HUGE! Since I'm crowding old age myself, in fact, they're much bigger than I am, but I continue twirling, caressing, and talking 'em up. All the time I'm doing that I'm inwardly questioning the sense of it all. Why would anyone put so much stock in something so fleeting after all. The average life span of a Christmas tree between the ax and the chipper is 2.1 weeks. But it's the interim, the sweet, nostalgia-packed interim that seems to matter so much.

A couple of my most memorable tree customers are two local girls with Martha Stewart taste and raw determination; Debbie and Dana require the two most perfect trees in the world and will stop at nothing to get them. Their impromptu arrival usually finds me in some kind of awkward place, like under a tractor with a grease gun in my hand or shoveling three feet of snow off a roof. It always starts in the same sing-songy way: "Oh hellooooo...we're back." Their radar zeros in on me, the most important person in their lives for the time being.

"Oh it's you again," I say, feigning gruffness, and then our dance begins. We head into our tree lot which I'm convinced will be a veritable desert to them. For the next hour, the three of us expend enough energy fluffing, poofing, twisting and turning trees to electrify Chicago for a month but nothing is quite right. I consider offering them each $10 if they'll go to the competition but at the end, those dreaded words spew out like an avalanche: "We'll be back after you cut some more." I look out over the beauties they've just rejected, knowing there's nothing better to cut, but they leave before I can protest. It usually takes them multiple visits and me a huge amount of scavenging but somehow I always find them the two best trees in the world.

My good wife, Betsy, helped me with the moral to this story. She listens to all my bitchin' about "people and their trees" but quickly passes it off. "You know, Burr, it's not really about the trees...it's the rituals and relationships." she says. She points out the pure joy Debbie and Dana share over their annual antics and the love between the couple who buy a big tree. I get the residuals of sharing friendship with these folks and knowing of the joy in their lives that I help provide. The trees just stand as a focal point for the relationships, big, small, filled out or ugly. And speaking of ugly: Betsy and I have developed a Christmas tree ritual ourselves—we always take home the one tree that doesn't sell. It stands rejected by all our customers, ugly as a bulldog and barely green. I grab it, light as a feather compared to all the huge ones I've handled, and take it to my home. We prop it up in a corner and place a few ornaments on it, where it smells great and reminds us of the joy of Christmas...a very special tree, it is.

Chapter 37

Our Russian Boy

BESIDES THE USUAL MAPLE sugaring paraphernalia, our sugarhouse contains a mishmash of old farming artifacts, piles of retired sap buckets, and sculptures fashioned from interesting shaped trees. It's intriguing to see the different tastes of people who go there. Some, bent only on learning about the maple process, gravitate to the evaporator and completely ignore everything else. The right-brained folks stop at the sculptures, and the antique-minded ogle over the artifacts. One thing that gets universal review, however, is a special stone that sits just outside the sugarhouse. It's an odd, pyramid-shaped stone that I picked out from a hedgerow of boulders on our farm. It serves to memorialize our Russian son, Alex, who loved the sugarhouse.

Alex came to us in the fall of 1994. We hadn't expected to host an international exchange student, but a friend of mine worked for World Learning and was putting the pressure on. We scanned a list of students from all over the world, thinking of the inadequacies of our small house and our busy schedules. Something, however, about a blond, round-faced boy from Kirov, Russia, spoke to Betsy, the family naysayer. His name was Alexey Eugenievich Novosyolov and she was drawn to his eyes; deep Russian eyes that we would grow to know so well.

We had no trouble picking him out from the group disembarking from the plane at Burlington International Airport. He was lankier than we had thought—stood a head taller than our two boys, who went to him and bashfully shook his hand. Betsy hugged him and asked if she might call him "Lexie." She looked bewildered—hurt even—as this strange boy shoved aside our attempts to help, picked up his entire luggage and said, "Call me Alex."

He was silent on the ride home, showing little interest in the Vermont countryside. When we pulled into our yard, he went purposefully to his luggage, once again brushing aside our attempts to help. It was not until suppertime that the ice broke. We were seated around the table, the three boys on one side. Betsy had made soup, which Alex attacked with a Russian vengeance. He cleaned his plate of the meat and potatoes but refused her offer of dessert with his longest dialogue yet: "I am full of it," he announced. Our boys, Rob and Tom, first looked at each other and then erupted into gales of laughter at this statement, packed with both Russian innocence and American double meaning! He appeared confused for only a second before a huge smile grew on his face and he joyfully pushed the two other boys, domino style, off their chairs. The bonding was complete.

Alex fit into our family like a Russian winter—intense, with a strong sense of belonging. He played hard and worked hard. He excelled at U-32 High School, as good with the classics as he was technology. Technology was his passion, however. We still have Alex repair jobs and devices in our house and on our farm. His talents, I might add, were not always practical or legal—there's a still somewhere in our neighborhood, still possibly cranking out vodka with Alex's name on it!

Our relationships took varied dimensions. With me he was light and jovial; he called me "Mr. Burr" and joked about my lack of hair and short stature (Mr. Burr's not fat—he just has a low center of gravity). He played music and pranks with our boys and learned American teenage things—above all, he was a loving brother. His serious side only came out with Betsy. Betsy helped him with schedules and studies; she wanted him to take the positive part of America back to Russia when he left us in June. Sometimes, late at night, Alex expressed his darker side to Betsy. He accepted the destiny of a short life and nothing Betsy said would assuage that feeling—he seemed to know.

We sent him home to Kirov in June when school ended, a boy with two faces. His Russian face returned to a country in turmoil and a home and heritage that he loved. His American face held a devilish grin and said goodbye with a pledge to meet again soon. He picked up the same bags he arrived with, now full with American stuff, and that's the last we saw of Alex. Four months later we received a call that he had witnessed a drug transaction in Kirov and been killed by the Russian mafia.

My story ends, also, with two faces. A sad face still grieves for Alex, our Russian son. A happier face, however, accepts the memories of fun and laughter. The memorial outside our sugarhouse prompts many questions about Alex. I've grown used to the queries but am not ruled by sadness. I prefer to think of Alex as not deceased. He's a fixer and a joker. He's led my family to Russia twice now where his people are ours and his presence is felt by us all. His presence is also in our sugarhouse by that pyramid-shaped stone. It's just a simple stone with a simple message but points to the sky where Alex beams back a bigger message: "Treat life like Russian meal—eat, be happy and walk away 'full of it'."

Chapter 38

Passing the Torch

IN THE WORLD OF WRITING, there's always a little discrepancy between the "pen and the personality"—not that I lie, mind you, but I'm never opposed to tweaking my writing to reveal myself a bit happier-go-lucky than I am. My father, Harry Morse, Sr., however, was truly happy-go-lucky and in love with every day. He was already a cup-half-full type when his auction in 1966 rendered him free of milking cows and ready to take on the world as a vegetable farmer. Add to that the suaveness of Rudolf Valentino and a natural theatrical bent, and it became Harry Morse's job to charm folks into coming to Morse Farm; it was my job to figure out what they wanted, make sure there was always plenty of it, and then stay out of the way.

During the thirty years Dad and I continued in this vein, I became a take-the-bull-by-the-horns worker, a Vermont-born Sisyphus, hand-picking his boulders and thinking he's the only one who could push them right. In the early days, that meant supplying perfect vegetables for folks even if I had to weed and pick by candlelight. Our major Christmastime product, however, had a nasty little added dimension: folks get downright personal about their Christmas trees. Getting the perfect one for everyone who came to Morse Farm became huge, but I was determined to succeed.

Last year I wrote a column about a couple of my "special needs" tree customers. This year the same two come back to mind like familiar but tattered ornaments from the attic dust. Debbie and Dana seek me out every year with their relentless search for the world's two most perfect Christmas trees. Dana recently e-mailed me a very well-written but vastly incomplete description of their needs:

> *Debbie likes a Frasier fir for her tree. She says there's something about Frasiers; they don't drop their needles all over the house, have sturdier branches so the ornaments don't fall like a marble in a pinball machine on its way to the floor, and sometimes they sprout new growth!*

Humph! I prefer a balsam for its traditional aroma, and larger girth!
When the ornaments tinkle through the floppy branches, I know
the holiday season is over and the tree needs to go!

To that, I say "Humph!" Those are just two criteria on their endless list of Yule tree demands that include fluffiness of the fir, shade of the green, angle of the stump, length of the bows, prickliness of the needles, how it will look after one inch is taken off to accommodate the angel, and the list keeps going on! In spite of all this folderol, I always find those two their perfect trees...that is until this year.

That's right...this year it ended just like that. You see, one day I was walking through my store when, all of a sudden, they appeared, grinning like maniacs, from behind a stack of maple syrup. The routine began the same old way:

"Hi Burrrrrr, we're heeeeere," they say in a sing-song fashion. "Oh, it's you again...suppose you want trees," I say, like the Grinch.

The next thing they said struck me like a stocking stuffed with reindeer poop. "Oh, don't you worry...Tommy's getting our treeeees...he knows just what we waaaaant."

I didn't say it before we parted that day but I gave Tommy a snowball's chance in hell of finding them suitable trees, but, lo and behold, he came to me later on and said they both loved the trees he cut and departed more giggly than ever. My son Tommy has been working at Morse Farm for four years; he wants to take over some day. It seems Tommy had greeted them in the yard, twirled tree after tree for them to reject, and finally suggested they come in the store to shop while he went out to cut some more. "Sounds like just the way I started out with those two," I thought. I also thought of the knock-down-drag-outs Tommy and I have had over my wanting him to do things just the way I would. "Debbie and Dana sure are tough cookies," he said, summing it up, "but I finally got 'em two trees that they loved."

His words struck me with a strange contrast of finality and relief; the finality of fifty-nine Christmas seasons that have come and gone in my life and the relief of knowing that Tommy can do it. Whew, I'm ready to pass the torch...heck no, I'll pass the whole evaporator! Thank you Debbie, Dana, and Tommy.

Chapter 39

Safe Reassurance

SOMETIMES IDEAS FOR these bi-weekly epistles are as scarce as hens' teeth, so when one sneaks up and taps me on the shoulder, I consider it a wonderful gift. That happened yesterday and the tap was as gentle as the warm breeze and the sea of buttercups that surrounded me at the time. I was mowing the meadow down in back of the barn with my new Japanese-made, orange tractor. The late June heat and the fragrance of new-mown hay brought memories of the good old days when my Grandpa Morse mowed the same land with his trusty Allis Chalmers Model B, also bright orange. I'm not comparing myself with Sidney Morse in any way except the color of our tractors and the nature of our task; he was much more a gentleman than I am! We were, however, best friends and had a certain spiritual alignment: two peas in a pod, so to speak.

One time he sensed my agony from a distance and stepped in, literally. It was early June and he was mowing that same meadow. I had just bounced off the school bus on the last day of school, excited about the summer ahead. A look down in the valley, however, put an instant damper on my excitement. From that distance I could just barely make out that orange tractor with a small crowd of people around it. It looked like there had been an accident and I started running toward it through the tall grass. It was slow going, much like running through deep snow, and I fell often. One time as I picked myself up I glanced through sweaty, pollen-filled eyes toward the still distant tractor. Someone was hurrying toward me and I knew it was Grandpa Morse from his gait. He walked like he spoke, soft and purposeful, almost as though his next step might be on water. We finally got within shouting distance and he spoke first:

"Everything's OK, Burr," he said. "I saw you get off the bus and knew you'd be worried."

When we met, he put his arm on my shoulder and explained that he had almost mowed into a spotted fawn lying in the grass and the crowd was just neighborhood folks gathered to look at it. We turned and walked toward the tractor, talking about our summer plans as we went. The people were just dispersing when we got there but the fawn still lay, unfazed, in a nest made by its absent mother. I felt lucky for myself and the fawn.

I'm reminded of another time someone approached me from a distance, this time under totally opposite circumstances. I was hanging out in a Holiday Inn in Los Angeles waiting for a plane. It was getting dusky when I started walking to a Mexican restaurant the front desk had recommended. Two revelations struck me as I entered under wide bridges that carried multiple lanes of I-405 through that part of town: One, that I had neglected to ask if it was a safe area to walk. Two, that there were two individuals coming toward me at the other end of the dark tunnel! Graffiti up at the bridge abutments highlighted whole neighborhoods of cardboard boxes—homes for the homeless. I knew from the shuffling gates of the two approaching me that they were not tourists. They intermittently jabbed at the air in boxer dances and kicked at cans and trash that littered the sidewalk. As they got nearer, I could see they sported oversized, straggly dreadlocks. My fright grew with the traffic noise, now directly above me. I knew there was no escape—too late for cutting and running. I hoped they would settle for my money and nothing else.

Finally, proximity verified my suspicions. They looked rougher than I had imagined. Their biceps bulged from sleeveless, tattered shirts and hosted big, ugly tattoos. One of them spat, just before turning in my direction. Training his dark eyes on my own, he spoke in a loud, ghetto voice: "Sir, Jesus loves you."

"That's it?" I thought, craning my neck and squeaking an anemic "thanks" to their backs. I continued on to the other side of the tunnel and the best Mexican meal I've ever had, very thankful that Jesus loves me. In spite of that warm, friendly thought, I called for a taxi to take me back to the hotel after my meal!

There are enough morals to this story to reach clear from Vermont to California, but the one I'm most partial to is this: There's a lot of faith and love in this world. Sometimes it appears with a spotted fawn and it's virtually guaranteed next door with a favorite grandpa. Sometimes, however, love and faith reach out in the most unexpected places. It may be in a foreign language in a ghetto or in the middle of the ocean, but when it comes, it feels as warm as if it happened in a sea of buttercups, right back home.

Chapter 40

Creative Road Work

OF ALL FOUR VERMONT seasons, spring is by far the most neurotic. The freezing and thawing that our beloved sugar season thrives on usually comes in the lower case but this year, I'll spell the words with capital letters: Freezing and Thawing. The Thawing has happened just enough to rut up our back roads and the Freezing has held those ruts in an indelible limbo, it seems, forever. My distant cousin, Julie Shafer from the wilds of Woodbury, recently e-mailed me with words of frustration: "Right now my road is a hazard and I wish the road crews would do something creative with the mix of ice and frozen mud ruts. Just to add to the misery, fresh falling snow covers the ice and ruts so you can't really see them." Reminds me of a harrowing experience I once had with a feeble attempt the road crew made to do something creative.

It was a spring similar to the one we're having this year and those deeply frozen ruts lay tangled like train tracks gone berserk. No doubt the phone up at the town garage rang off the hook with complaints but there was nothing the road crew could do but dump a little gravel, create a little psychology, and pray for pea season. That year, however, nature gave them a little edge on the psychology angle; one day, it started spitting snow and didn't stop till six inches lay on those roads. They attacked the storm with the only tool worth its salt in such situations, the town grader. Their intentions, I'm sure, were to remove the snow but instead the huge machine worked like a big drywall trowel, depositing snow down into the ruts and leaving a smooth appearance on top.

I was on the volunteer fire department at that time and one crispy night we got called to a chimney fire over at the Perkins place in the Horn of the Moon. It was sugar season and our old Jeep pickup truck was piled clear to the top of its high sideboards with slab wood for the evaporator. My car was broken down so I jumped into the Jeep, slammed the sagging door shut, and headed out. The Cummings Road had not been graded so

I drove slowly over its snow-covered ruts, knowing that the Jeep's brittle springs would break easily under the weight of the slabs. When I turned right onto North Street, silhouettes of the Worcester Mountains loomed majestically in the moonlit sky; the combination of adrenaline and nature's beauty gave me a late-night rush. As I turned left onto Sparrow Farm Road, I noticed the surface was smooth and neat. It resembled a beautiful white ribbon that curved downhill toward the Sparrow Farm and points west. I was almost euphoric, ready to take on the fiercest of chimney fires. The Jeep purred along like a satisfied old she-cat so I dropped her right down into high gear and let her go. The farm buildings zoomed past on my left and then the road curved slightly northwest.

Suddenly the truck lurched to the right and then back to the left. "What the hell," I thought, just before my years of mud-season driving brought me back to reality. I remembered the area ahead would be a sea of ruts—this time frozen ruts troweled over to look like a beautiful white ribbon. I prepared for the ride of my life, knowing that it might also be my last ride. The Jeep went up on two wheels, settled back and then went onto the other two. Inside the cab, I jounced around like a Styrofoam peanut in a squirrel cage fan, fearing that I would be thrown out, or worse, end up under an aged pickup and its cargo of sawmill waste. Somehow I made it to the bottom of the hill where I knew the ruts would end but success was not to be; the Jeep made a final lurch into a gully, raised up one last time, and laid over on its side. I heard the slabs spill out like a giant game of pick-up-sticks.

It took me several minutes to realize I was going to be OK and I climbed out the driver's door which now opened up toward the nighttime sky. By then my fellow firemen were driving by and the first of them slowed to ask if I was alright. "I'm OK," I hollered. "Go ahead...I'll get there." By the time I had walked the rest of the way to the chimney fire, it had been put out and the firemen were leaving. The next day, I took the farm tractor over, uprighted the Jeep, and restacked the slabs into its bed. I'll never blame the town crew for the situation that night. After all, they were just trying to do something "creative" with the spring roads. I feel sorry for road crews in the spring; they walk a fine line between knowing there's nothing they can do and answering to irate taxpayers. And as for the irate taxpayers, I would advise them to suck it up, realize there are a few things that money can't buy and pray a lot—pray for pea season.

Chapter 41

Sunless Places

THE OTHER DAY LIFE gave me a look at the concept of keepin' it under your hat versus spillin' the beans. It started off with a trip to the hospital to get some blood drawn for a prostate PSA check. Modern medicine has done a wonderful job of providing various alarms for life- threatening diseases, and hospitals, the muscle of modern medicine, do a wonderful job, too. I just wish they could stay out of the business of information control, a process that incurs huge overhead but is absolutely doomed to fail.

At the hospital, there was a short wait at the first checkpoint where several of us sat elbow to elbow. Talk flowed as naturally as water toward—what else?—what ailed us. My number was called quickly, but not before the entire group was intimately familiar with my prostate. I was sent to a hallway lined with multiple cubbies that resembled church confessionals but were for a hugely different purpose; in church you tell all to God's hotline—at the hospital, not even God is supposed to know. I reported to Station 3 where a receptionist accepted all the numbers, street addresses, and dotted i's that could positively indict my insurance company, my checkbook, and anyone else who might be in line to pay. When I left, I entered a second waiting area. I sat next to an older man who looked like he would, in any other setting, be concerned with the weather.

"What you here for, son?" he asked

"Prostate."

"Say what?"

"PROSTATE!"

A room full of wide-eyed people suddenly interrupted their discussions about each other's ailments to focus on my midsection. My conversation with the older man went on, at high volume, to his eighty-seven-year collection of health problems until my name was finally called by a comely young lady in hospital garb. She led me into the next room where I recited yet more vital statistics before proffering my bare arm for an efficient and painless blood drawing. As I departed past those same folks in the waiting room, I felt branded by that chestnut-sized gland that lies in my innards close to where the sun don't shine.

My next stop was the Wayside Restaurant for a post—blood-drawing breakfast. I sat down at the counter and had hardly got my hat off when a man opposite me shouted: "Burr, I heard you're havin' prostate trouble." A half-dozen diners turned in my direction, eating utensils in midair. "It's OK," I said, trying to zero-in my voice just on him. "It's just a simple blood test. I'm fine." I marveled at the microworld between the hospital waiting room and the Wayside Restaurant—reminds me of a story my friend, John Lamberton, lumber sawyer and ace storyteller, told of the early days of telephone when there were no secrets anywhere.

It seems Nate Flint, owner of a local sawmill, always said what was on his mind in a loud voice no matter where he was or whose company he was in. One time he got upset at the telephone operator and told her to "shove the telephone up *** ***" (and the deleted words have, of course, to do with that same old sunless place). The phone people had warned Nate about his language before and this put them over the edge. The manager of the telephone company got right in his car and went to Flint's sawmill. He stormed into Nate's office and announced he was there to take the phone out...said the only way he could leave it in was if Nate would call the operator and apologize for his remarks. Nate Flint went immediately to the phone and when the operator came on said, "Are you the woman I told shove the phone up her ***?" The woman indignantly replied that she was, expecting a heartfelt apology. "Well," Nate said, "You better get ready 'cause they're comin' with it now!"

John didn't say if Nate Flint ever got his telephone back, but he sure did live in a simpler world. Back then hospitals lacked PSA tests and human ailments often went undetected. That's the upside of hospitals today. The downside is that they're still dealing with the same old humans who live and talk freely. Speaking of which, my doctor recently told me my PSA was low; guess all's well with me for the time being down there where the sun don't shine. Shhhh...the hospital thinks no one else knows.

Chapter 42

Trust in the Spring

WE'VE BEEN MERCHANTS up here at Morse Farm ever since 1966 when my father sold out, lock, stock and milkin' machine. In his terms, he'd "borrowed" from those cows long enough and was ready to try his hand at "milkin'" the species Homo sapiens. Harry Morse loved jokin' around and always had a good time with the folks who stopped at our place; they laughed off his innuendoes and supported our store generously. Jokin' around is different these days, though. Certain words and ways that used to be just part of the culture are taboo today, like Harry Morse's term, "borrowing." He figured anything renewable, like sap from the maple trees, crops from the soil, or milk from the cows was really just borrowing. Sadly, folks these days are changing the way they think about the commercialization of those things.

I feel lucky to be in the business of retailing maple products because it's a trade that has not fallen victim to outsourcing or mass-marketing by places like Wal-Mart (does anyone really want to buy maple syrup from Wal-Mart?). In fact, when folks visit our sugarhouse, they are accepting of the old ways, including a few jokes and mild cuss words...must be something in the sap water we've been borrowing. The other day a group from a distant state came in. They looked with awe at the old, rustic sugarhouse, some, no doubt, expecting to see a huge factory just crankin' out maple syrup. They settled in for my show, which includes a reference to our eight generations of Morse maple sugar makers. After they left the sugarhouse, they went to our store and shopped...happily, I might add. Before they got back on their bus, they congregated out front and I mingled with them for a few minutes. I always like to ask folks about their world—where they're from, what they're up to. I found out that they were all members of the same Christian church in the Midwest, self-proclaimed born againers they were.

It was a beautiful day and the conversation led in various directions. In spite of the bucolic surroundings, I allowed that running my business brings the typical challenges of the times, including the ins and outs of passing it on to the next generation. They asked the names of my sons and I told them that Tommy, my youngest, wants to take the business over some day. I was surprised when one of them asked if they could pray with me. "Sure," I said. "Why not?" Suddenly a half-dozen of us were in a circle, heads bowed, listening to a Midwest farm guy talk to God. He addressed the beauty around us, including the clean air, the abundance of maple trees, and the water that flows freely. He also asked God to bless Tommy's future at Morse Farm.

I'll admit to feeling a tad bit strange at the scenario and lifting my head once to peek. There, standing close by, was Daniel Antonovich, our local water entrepreneur, with eyes as big as the bottom of a small tumbler. Dan owns the Montpelier Springs, a mecca on the hill above our farm where a small river of ice-cold water has belched from the earth and flowed away to the North Branch River for thousands of years. He wants to get permission to bottle a portion of that water to satisfy a thirsty populace, but there are folks saying "No way...water belongs to everyone and you can't sell it." I feel for Daniel because he bought a resource, like maple trees or tillage, but stands to lose its value. After the prayer ended and my new friends headed for their bus, Daniel, a trusted colleague and neighbor, approached me. "That was a sight to behold," he said, touched by the scene and the words of prayer. His exit words, "That's how folks used to be," sounded an alarm to me; I wished he hadn't used the past tense like that. I know that changes are always necessary, but I still pine for the olden days before "political correctness," when talk and prayer were freer and a neighbor could bottle up some water for the thirsty... "and the streams of living water will flow." (John 7:28)

Chapter 43

Water Water Everywhere

"WATER, WATER EVERYWHERE and, by golly, I'm not even thirsty." I've modified that old adage to accommodate two truths that I'll start this story with. One, that I live on a farm filled with babbling brooks, bubbling springs, and wet spots that swallow whole tractors; two, that I'm rarely thirsty, an enigma in this community where folks would sooner be without their arms and legs than their water bottles. By all accounts, in fact, I should be dead. The word is that we need to drink our weight in water every day, or some such thing, or face dire health consequences. My mother, who recently passed away at ninety, hated water and never drank a drop. She believed that flowers, love, and Brownie Supremes are much more necessary to life than water.

Judging by what I've said so far, you might think that I, too, have no use for the stuff, but that is far from correct. I bathe every day in water, boil sap that's ninety-eight percent water and, most especially, have a spiritual link to water. I've been fascinated with dowsing ever since I was a toddler watching my father find long-lost water pipes and underground streams with a forked apple stick. Dowsers, aka "water witches," in my book are much closer to truth, God, and the American way than just about anyone. Speaking of truth, I must make a painful admission at this point: dowsing never has worked for me.

A few days ago I was down popping maple kettle corn at the Vermont Water Week celebration on the statehouse lawn. On break, I wandered over to the dowsers station, wistfully thinking of the times I'd held a forked stick in my hands to dismal avail. I approached a young man with "John" on his nametag and said that I was very interested in the art but had never been able to do it. "He's the one you need to work with," John said with a tone of reverence, pointing to a large man with his back to us. The man wore a wide- brimmed straw hat and around his waist hung a holster overflowing with dowsing tools. My mind went creative: "Able to swim the English Channel with a single stroke...finds water where no one has found it before...look...down in the depths...It's a fish. It's a submarine. It's AQUAMAN!" John stepped over and tapped the big man on the shoulder and when he swiveled, my anticipation of a square-jawed hero deflated like a punctured rubber raft: AQUAMAN turned out to be my neighbor, Barry Langer!

Barry and I shook hands and I told him my story. He pulled two divining rods (wire rods bent at right angles) from his holster, handed them to me, and told me to hold them pointing straight ahead and imitate a sleepwalking trance. He said they would turn in my hands when I reached a vein of water. He pointed to a flagged line where he had previously located a vein 160 feet down and I slowly headed toward it. I crossed the line and went slightly beyond. Nothing. I did it again. Nothing. Repeated trials and prompting by Barry brought nary a twitch from those rods, despite my positive answer to Barry's question, "Do you believe?" (and I do...I believe...I BELIEVE!). Barry had to interrupt our session for a group of school kids who wanted to try dowsing. He first gave them a cursory lesson and then sent them toward the line. Their rods, without exception, pivoted like dutiful little soldiers when they reached the vein of water! I left dejected and went back to making popcorn.

I returned later in the day for one final attempt. Barry was busy, but I helped myself to some rods on the table. I tried harder than ever to follow Barry's instructions and think of water flowing through the earth 160 feet down but the rods refused to budge. A woman named Lisa came up to me and said she had been watching and wanted to help. She refused to accept my inability, even after witnessing several more failed attempts. She led me to an isolated place on the statehouse lawn—said she was going to "clear me of negative energy." It was a beautiful day and I was glad to follow her instructions to lie down and relax. She started at my feet and, although my eyes were closed, I sensed her hands hovering over me in a gentle dough-kneading fashion, drawing out those little negative buggers like magnets draw iron filings. Somewhere in the fog of total relaxation, I heard a small voice intone, "Is that man dead?" I opened my eyes just enough to see a mother quickly leading the lad away. When Lisa finished, I got up, feeling very relaxed and, yes, void of negative energy.

My story ends much the way it began, with water—"Water, water everywhere and, by golly, I'm not even thirsty." You see, when Lisa handed me the rods again, I fully expected I'd find water quicker than a fisherman finds it on Saturday morning. A stroll to the flag line netted the same old, same old but it was five feet beyond the line when I felt, for the first time in my life, those wonderful appliances swiveling in my hands. Lisa said the delayed reaction was no problem because water is water and I had, indeed, found a vein — my water vein. I thought of the stars above and all the attention they get just because, I suppose, they twinkle. Earth's water somehow gets ignored and forgotten, but not always. I walked away that day elated with the age-old art of dowsing and that I had found my vein. Barry and Lisa told me about the American Society of Dowsers, which is headquartered in Danville, Vermont. You know, by golly, I may join—yes I may, not because I'm a seasoned practitioner, but because I have the most important qualification — I BELIEVE.

Part Three

Sour & Sweet

Chapter 44

Balanced Travel

I'VE OFTEN MENTIONED our packaged "deal on wheels"—the folks who come to Morse Farm in huge tour buses. We love folks on buses, not just because of the economic blessings, but also because they are mostly charming and interesting people. It recently occurred to me, however, that I've been slighting a whole segment of the traveling population—those who cruise up County Road and into our parking lot on motorcycles. Motorcycle folks are fun and I speak without a smattering of profit motive because motor-cycle folks can't buy much of anything; they can't take it with them.

One memorable motorcycle visitor this summer was a bit of a bigwig. Peter Pantuso, president of the American Bus Association, came rumbling in one day along with his entourage of Vermont tourism officials. I had been tipped off that they were all traveling in this unorthodox manner and would be visiting me. I watched as the riders, appearing more like leath-ery motorcycle appendages, pulled into our yard, parked side by side, and flicked off the rumbling. They set their kickstands, dismounted, and began peeling and snapping off motorcycle garb. Only then did personalities fa-miliar to me emerge, plus a heavy-set, middle-aged man who turned out to be Peter, CEO of 39,068 motor coaches that travel 2.444 billion miles a year in the USA.

I showed them how we entertain folks from 450 of those motor coaches each year at Morse Farm and treated them to some sticky sugar-on-snow. Mr. Pantuso, a true gentleman, asked questions like any of our Morse Farm visitors. They were on a tight schedule, so after a quick perusal of our store (and, sure enough, they couldn't buy much of anything), they went back out to their bikes. I followed them out, but just before I bade them good-bye, I commented about how ironic it was for the big man in charge of the buses to be touring on a motorcycle. In mock concern, Mr. Pantuso thrust his finger up to his lips and lowered his voice, "Don't tell anyone." I watched as they donned their motorcycle garb, flicked the rumbling back to life, and headed down the road, glad to have met the bus czar who can think outside of the box.

Another motorcycle encounter ended up being just as friendly but much scarier. Betsy and I were watering the plants one day when I looked up and saw two folks approaching on a single motorcycle. Just as they turned into our yard, the big bike suddenly tipped and its two occupants spilled onto the gravel surface like two rag dolls. We rushed over, thinking they might be badly hurt. "Are you OK?" Betsy asked, while I braced myself against the heavy machine which was leaking gasoline and threatening to roll on them. By that time they were both stirring and indicating that they were OK. They slowly stood and a shedding of helmets revealed a man and a woman, both sixtyish and wearing the extra pounds most of us do at that age. By that time, several people had gathered and four of us raised the motorcycle upright and wheeled it to a parking spot.

We learned that they were from Colorado; he had ridden the whole way and she had flown into Burlington, where he had just picked her up. They were headed from our place to the coast of Maine and then down to Baltimore, where they had friends. They stayed at our place for an hour, giving Betsy and me a chance to get to know them. We followed them out to their motorcycle when they left. I shuddered as they headed slowly down the road. Nearby, a tour bus was loading up, also bound for the coast of Maine. I wished our new friends from Colorado could be on it.

My third motorcycle story is pure delight. I was telling my friend, Chip, about the Coloradoan's mishap in our parking lot and he reported an incident he saw last year on the Appalachian Gap. Chip said it was a beautiful day and he had stopped at the summit overlook, just to soak in the view. He heard a group of motorcycles approaching from the Bristol side. When they got to the top, they turned into the overlook. He said the lead rider pulled up to park, following the usual parking procedure. The problem was, the lot has a deceptive little slope to it.

"He was so transfixed with the view," Chip said, "that when he set his kickstand, gravity took a rude turn for the worse. When he lowered the cycle, the deceptive little slope brought it beyond the balance point. All of a sudden the big bike, driver and all, tipped over."

Chip went on to describe the other motorcycles pulling up and doing the same thing. He said the place was littered that day with macho riders and their expensive machines, spilled about like toppled dominoes. Chip said they were unhurt but angry as hornets and twice as embarrassed!

I've always wanted a motorcycle, but the combination of age and schedule seems to be pointing against it. That's probably for the best. At my age and girth, gravity gets compounded and I guess my attraction to the earth is much better served on two feet or four wheels.

Chapter 45

Bottoms Up

HERE IT IS, HOT SUMMER again, the time of year when the personalities of cold drinks vary from the expensive restaurant fare with little umbrellas on top to bland cups of Kool-Aid from a child's roadside stand. When all is said and done, there's nothing better than a cold drink of water to fill the bill, but this season brings such creativity in the quality of quenching that I've decided to focus this column on a couple of home-brew experiences. The first one takes place in our sugarhouse where, with all the bus tours we get, I've become a student of group psychology.

In our slide show, we mix in some local color with hard facts about the Vermont maple process, enough to get most groups stimulated and involved. Although there is an occasional group that's just plain dull, most are a pure joy to behold, and there's nothing any more fun than a group with an individual who stimulates some light sparring with a witty comment. A while back I had a bus full of Irishmen and I could see by their faces that they were loaded to fire. I hadn't gone too far when one piped up and said, "Ye've got to be driven to drink wi' work that hard!" Without missing a beat, I risked my best attempt at an Irish brogue: "Ahhh a man after me own hearrrt." Laughter filled the sugarhouse and in the blink of a leprechaun's eye, the tone had been set to the subject of "the drink."

My show went on to a picture of the neighbor's sugarhouse steaming away into a moonlit night sky. "He's been accused of makin' something besides maple syrup," I said. "Aye...moonshine...ye got any?" chorused the crowd. At that point a guy piped up, "Would ye be wantin' me t'send ye a liter in the post?" His ruddy face and black, bulbous nose suggested that he was a seasoned expert on the subject of alcohol. "Hmmmm...that's very kind of you, sir, but it would be way too expensive," I said, feeling my guts burn at the thought.

"It'll be no bother," he persisted. "Maybe ye would trade for one of yer books." (My brother always starts the show by greeting folks on the buses and mentioning my book, *Sweet Days & Beyond*).

"I don't know," I posed to my audience, "should I trust him?"

The answer came from multi-directions and was as clear as a pint of Guinness: "What ayre ye thinkin'...he's from Limerick, you know!"

The rest of my show went off without a hitch but the man approached me later on in our store with the same offer. For some strange reason I suddenly found myself closing the deal: one of my books for a liter of something illegal, caustic to the innards, and receivable at the whim of a stranger. That happy group of Irishmen shopped for souvenirs and small sizes of our famous liquid—maple syrup—and when they boarded their bus, I shook hands and bid them a cheerful goodbye. Their visit is now a distant memory and that package hasn't arrived yet. I'm waiting with baited breath, though, not because I have an appetite for the stuff, but because I'm craving an answer to the puzzle they left me with: Where on the honesty scale do folks from Limerick lie?

Sweltering July days bring back memories of a much more puritanical home brew—root beer, wonderful summertime root beer. Oh how I loved cracking the tops of those bottles and guzzling it almost by the gallon. It was a family affair that started with lots of hoarded quart-size soda bottles, Domino Sugar almost by the dump truck load, and a little magical liquid called Root Beer Extract. On brewing day, we mixed it all up with fresh spring water, funneled the black liquid into each quart bottle, and sealed them with real soda bottle caps, applied by a special capping tool. I'll always remember my pride in thinking it was a recipe only our family knew and that my friends would wonder how we got the caps on.

The only painful part of the process was waiting the two weeks while that wonderful elixir aged in our attic; —that is, till the year we made our infamous last batch. That year our water started tasting different just before the root beer was completely aged. After a few days of it, our father went up to the springhouse to see what might be wrong. There, in the spring, he found an unfortunate woodchuck that had somehow broken through the cover and fallen in. Dad came home holding his stomach and saying we needed to abstain from drinking that water for a long time, but the worst part was when he ordered us to dump the root beer, bottle by painful bottle, down the drain. Yes, the woodchuck episode rendered our home brewing days over and to this day, every time I see the words "root beer" I think of both putrefied woodchucks and that wonderful summertime brew that tasted so good.

The world holds a veritable reservoir of thirst-quenching ideas and the two I mentioned today are hardly bottoms-up situations. It's strange how humans always try to one up the best drink of all—cold spring water—with all sorts of concoctions that are bad for the health. Sure, the sugary drinks taste good and the alcoholic drinks feel good but there's always safety in water—that is, if the spring's got a tight cover.

Chapter 46

My Favorite Briar Patch

NOW THAT FOLIAGE SEASON is over, I've taken a few opportunities lately to look off and savor the view out in front of our place. It's truly beautiful. With all the complications of travel these days, it kinda makes me wonder why anyone would ever want to leave a place like this. My wife, Betsy, feels the same. One day last week she was out in the yard under a sky that was bluer than blue; the dog was frolicking through her piles of leaves, the temperature was perfect, and they were both high as the puffy white clouds on life here in East Montpelier. She was so high on nature that she insisted that her wheelchair-bound mother be in on the joy. When she hurried into the house to get her, the telephone was ringing.

To fully understand the rest of this story, I must point out that Betsy's a bit of an oddity in today's world of telecommunication—she refuses to have an answering machine. Her attitude is that phones are there to be answered or not to be answered. For some odd reason, even though the indoors repelled her that day, she answered the phone. It started out with a long hesitation, like whoever was on the other end could not believe a real person had answered.

"Eese theese Harvey Mahris?" a young, female voice asked.

"No, this is not Harry Morse," Betsy replied, painfully ennunciating my real name.

"Eese theese Meeses Harvey?"

"Yes," Betsy said, giving up on elocution and, for that matter, accuracy, honesty and sanity, still filled with East Montpelier euphoria.

"Meeses Harvey...theese eese Consuela frommm Heeelton Hotel...how are jew?"

"I'm wonderful!" Betsy said, loading to fire with a plan.

Another long hesitation (Consuela had not been programmed for that response)."OK. Meeses Harvey...I have great news for jew today...I can geeve jew Las Vegas for only..."

"Las Vegas!" Betsy roared. "Mercy sakes, Consuela, why would anyone want to go there? I'm from Vermont, the most beautiful place in the world. Have you ever been to Vermont?"

"Jew don't understand, Meeses Harvey, eets the treepe of the santury!"

"Oh Consuela...I couldn't accept...you're sooooo nice, but let's talk about Vermont...let's see...I could even pick you up at the airport..."

"No Meeses Harvey," Consuela giggled. "Jew don't understand...what about Orlando...Orlando eese yours for..."

"Oh gracious no, deary...you're a sweetheart but I'd never go to Orlando...it's a dreadful place. Say...when you come to Vermont, why don't you just plan on staying with us..."

"Sorry Meeses Harvey," Consuela giggled again. "I theenk I have another call."

"Oh, don't hang up, Consuela...we're just getting to know each other," Betsy implored just before a click and an obnoxious buzzing freed her to go back into the yard.

Betsy related the scenario saying it was all about the rabbit and the briar patch. When I questioned her rationale, she said that in the story the rabbit outwitted the fox by suggesting an end that was totally unreasonable to the fox but perfect for the rabbit. In the terms of these ridiculous telescammers and their trained monkeys, the Las Vegases and the Orlandos are Gardens of Eden ala Gold Card. For Betsy, however, they are places only fit for hungry foxes. She's looking forward to a long winter right here in Vermont, the briar patch she loves.

Chapter 47

The Road from Cabin Fever

AHHH...SPRING IN VERMONT...take a deep breath, a deep, deep breath, and if you think I'm talkin' about the sweet smell of syrup you'd be barkin' up the wrong maple tree. I'M TALKIN' ABOUT CABIN FEVER...NOW BREATHE DEEP AND EVERYTHING WILL BE FINE! Whew — sorry folks, but sometimes it's frantic and a bit whacked out this time of year.

Take my friend, Susan, over at the Mad River Valley Chamber of Commerce, for instance: right now she's upset about the terminology of frost heaves. She claims they've started calling them "bumps" and she's upset.

"As a Vermonter, I am kind of insulted by that," she says. "Frost Heave signs mean that a special bump is ahead, not one due to poor road maintenance, but a *special* bump. Frost Heave signs are like an award given at the end of the long winter season, you know? They take on personality, those Frost Heaves." (Note how she capitalizes them like they're people...pitiful...pitiful). She continues: "You go through Duxbury on Route 100 and some years you can get some really good 'uns. Some are wimpy, some are impressive. Bumps are a nuisance because they never go away, but Frost Heaves make a grand entrance, and once thoroughly enjoyed, quietly fade away."

Susan's never actually admitted it to me but I know she talks to them and I can just imagine the conversation:

"You feisty devil, you—looks like you got up on the wrong side of the bedrock this morning—haw, haw. Oh darnit, you made me spill my coffee again. Ohhhhh BOY, I TOLD YOU YESTERDAY—ONE MORE TIME AND I'D REPORT YOU TO THE HIGHWAY DEPARTMENT FOR SEISMIC HARASSMENT!"

The good news about cabin fever is that, like Frost Heaves, it does go away. A little fresh maple syrup is the perfect antidote even in extreme cases like Susan's. Today I went over to the East Montpelier Town Meetin' kind of lookin' for a fight—I've got a little low-grade CF myself, you know. I drove very slowly on the way over; a lack of snow, coupled with Arctic temperatures has begat Biblical Frost Heaves and I knew of one gunnin' for me where the brook crosses Dodge Road.

The first agenda item at Town Meetin' 06 was a $2.5 million dollar school budget. It passed with flying colors by voice vote without a sign of debate. In fact, I almost voiced the single "nay" vote just for the entertainment factor but, instead, sat there nodding my head and looking satisfied like everyone else. Passage of the $2.5 million led to an article for $100,000, which, like the school budget, passed soundly, but required an hour of heated debate. Town Meetin' was recessed for lunch on the dot of noon. Lunch is the best part of the day, a time when liberals and conservatives can sit and break bread instead of each other. The afternoon session brought EXCRUCIATING debate over several small articles—you know, $10,000 here and $18,000 there. I sensed a trend: as the dollar amounts of each ensuing article dropped, the debate increased. "Hmmm, very interesting," I thought, feeling a fight coming on. At the end, all passed after repeated reminders that each would only increase the grand list by one cent. Ahhh magic words!

The East Montpelier Town Meetin' is held in the school auditorium, a place designed for basketball not acoustics. That, I suppose, was the reasoning for the PA system, which nearly provided the fight I expected. Every once in a while it sounded a deafening, electrical wail, as if thumbing its nose at certain remarks. That, in turn, had the same effect on 150 nerve-wracked sufferers of cabin fever as a Tasmanian Devil loose in the hall. I felt sorry for the moderator who had to beg everyone to come up and use the feared microphone. He blamed it on legality rather than the acoustics, but held firm with every soul. Now, there's lots to be said for the average East Montpelier voter but "on a par with Wayne Newton in front of a microphone" is not on the list. The microphone stood on a telescoping stand, in a funnel-shaped holder. Its user-friendly design was immediately lost on 99 percent of the citizenry that day. Tall folks stooped. Short folks stretched and folks in-between held the cone-shaped mic like a rabbit holds a carrot, with two quivering paws...in the headlights! I had decided to physically attack the next person who shouted "hold the mic closer to your mouth" when the meetin' ended; saved by the gavel, we were. There were no meltdowns or fistfights. All told we spent over $3 million and were good for another year. I left feeling glad to have done my civic duty but still fragile with cabin fever.

As I drove home, up past Fairmont Farm and west on Dodge Road, I sunk into an exhausted daze. At the point where the brook crosses I realized, too late, that my speed was excessive. Suddenly my grey Nissan did a poor impression of Hannah Teter doing a quadruple alley-oop. When I finally got it under control, I turned the steering from side to side and checked the brakes. Everything seemed OK so I nudged the accelerator and resumed my drive home. Glancing in the rearview mirror at the receding countryside, I saw the cause of my trauma: a high gravelly mound in the road—a Frost Heave. "You got me good that time, you son of a gun," I said. My thoughts turned back toward straightening the bumps, so to speak, in town affairs. I knew I needed a drink...a drink of maple syrup.

Chapter 48

The Dog Days of Summer

SOMETIMES I WISH I HAD a more aggressive personality and often think of the opportunities I've missed by not stepping up and asserting myself more. The other day I got a chance to compare a couple of different personalities; they happened to be dogs, but since dogs are almost human, I say "What the heck?" It started with an early morning walk through the August dew. Averill, a black Lab responded to my invitation to go for a swim with several jet-propelled laps around the rug and a pink, sloppy tongue in my face. I love Averill in spite of our differences in personality; she's Type A clear to the bones and I'm a Type B. Averill led me to my car, falling just short of opening the door and starting it up. We drove down the road to a gray farmhouse where we had a date with Tia, a pit bull mix whose temperament wonderfully belies her genetics. Tia, another Type B, had to think twice before she came out of the house, but she had been left alone for the weekend by her roommates and really needed a bathroom break.

As the three of us headed down through the pasture from the farmhouse, Averill led Tia in frenzied circles like two black specks in a vortex. Every once in a while Averill would bounce up in my face with the message "Isn't life wonderful...it doesn't get any better than this!" Tia and I agreed, but less profusely. In the distance we saw our neighbor, Chip Stone, walking with his black Lab, Harbor. Harbor carries a few extra pounds and sports a gray beard these days. He exchanged pleasantries with Averill and Tia while Chip and I talked about people stuff, but he made it plain that he was neither up for a swim or any young dog deviltry. We said our goodbyes, Chip and Harbor going north, and Averill, Tia and I continuing south to our farm pond.

Averill, the retriever, is a swimmer supreme. Averill, the Type A, does a mean cannonball. She's taught me that when we get within stick throwin' distance from the pond, I best find a stick and throw it, which I did. Off she sprinted, hurling herself in the pond like a crazed teenager. *KERSPLASH!* Instantly she became a black head in a frothy wake, puffing and snorting. She clamped the stick like a snapping turtle and delivered it to me for repeat performances as long as my energy held out. Tia, on the other hand, approached the water much like I do, slowly, one foot at a time. At the pond's edge she found interest in frogs and other creatures that dwell among the cattails and swale grass. I tried to coax her into deep water but she wanted nothing to do with it.

When I finally tired of Averill's game, I called for the dogs to follow me. Averill gladly climbed to the bank, shook cold water all over me and the surrounding countryside, and rushed ahead. Tia, however, would not budge from her padding sweeps around the pond's edge. I thought she would eventually follow, so Averill and I headed up the path toward home. When Tia still ignored my calls, several hundred feet up the path, I asked Averill to go get her. The rest of my story is God's honest truth...

Averill looked at me, cocked her head like dogs do, and bounded back toward the pond. I hurriedly followed, wondering if this was the real Lassie moment it seemed to be. I crossed the bridge that leads up to the pond's berm and witnessed something that amazed me: Averill paddled out to where Tia was, touched the tip of her nose with her own, swiveled her head in a beckoning way, and paddled back out. Tia followed like a dutiful soldier...those two communicated just like two people (well...better than most people do)!

Averill's genius status was short lived, however. The next day Averill and I were riding with Betsy in her car over on Barnes Road, just around the corner from our farm. For some reason Betsy was only driving twenty miles per hour. It was a beautiful day and Averill hung out the window, as dogs will do. All of a sudden she and I spotted a huge gray squirrel at the edge of a driveway; I felt her stiffen as if preparing to lunge but just knew my genius dog wouldn't do that...I was wrong! She landed like a ski jumper-gone-wrong, rolling over three times and skidding along the loose gravel. She finally stopped, dazed but unhurt, at the base of a tree under a low limb where Mr. Squirrel sat laughing.

Yes, life gives us all plenty of opportunity to blow our genius status like Averill did with the squirrel. I've got several little diversions that instantly dwarf my IQ, too. Some might consider my habit of treating dogs on a par with humans one of them, but I don't care; dogs are wonderful beings and in many ways, more sensitive, personable, and, yes, smarter than people. I've got lots of friends and you've just met three of them, Averill, Tia, and Harbor. I love those guys and wish them big slurpy cheers in all they do.

Chapter 49

Fences Make Good Roads

WHEN IT COMES RIGHT DOWN to it, there's not a whole lot of difference between seafarers and Vermont landlubbers this time of year. That's right, our countryside has been as up and down lately as the highest of ocean swells. We go from winter wonderland to dense mud fields and then back to winter wonderland—sometimes all within twenty-four hours. There are, of course, drawbacks to both of these neurotic personalities. Walking with snowshoes presents the usual problems of sinking in deeply with each step and snowshoes that keep falling off unless they are adjusted with surgical care. Mud, of course, is mud—there're few redeeming qualities to a countryside full of slimy, sucking sludge that follows you into homes and wreaks havoc on marriages. But don't totally despair—there's hope for springtime optimists and kids at heart. Lately, we've been getting a great ride from the settling snow. Every once in a while, as we trudge along, a patch of snow the area of a barn roof will settle underneath. Our ride starts with a giant whoosh, and ends with a dizzying feeling equal to the best Tilt-a-Whirl ride and it's a heck of a lot cheaper!

As we proceed through this climatalogical neurosis toward sugarin's end, nature's never opposed to throwing us a frigid curve ball. Yesterday it was so cold that the woods turned into a shooting gallery. All around us, frozen trees popped and cracked like guns as we went about our tree-tapping business—kinda fun, it was! Tomorrow, however, may be a totally different story. No sugar season ever, ever escapes the mud, but mud doesn't have to be all bad. We have a place on our driveway where the world turns to Jell-O when mud gets just right. It shimmies and rolls and I love to go there and bounce. Sometimes I invite a friend to stand opposite me so that when I go down, he goes up, and we both walk away giggling.

There are places where nature's neurosis, however, can't be tolerated. Man continues attempting to take control, usually with dismal success. There are, however, occasional success stories and some of those occur in the swampy valleys that our gravel roads run through. My friend, Rockie Kelley, who grew up just up the road from me, explained:

"Back when cars took over where sleighs left off, the town road crews offered to swap modern barbed-wire fencing to the farmers for their stone walls."

Rockie explained that the flat slate stones, applied with equal amounts of Yankee ingenuity and bull strength, were the only cure for the worst of the springtime muddy spots. The farmers, on the other hand, found modern barbed wire much better fencing for their expanding herds of cows. Rockie was just a boy when he worked on the road crew. He said they first hand-excavated the muck and took it away. Then they picked up the stones from the farmers' walls with lumber wagons.

"Three pounders worked abreast," he said. "I worked between two older guys and our job was to set the stone [in traditional lingo, stone is plural] upright and pound them so that they seated into the ground a little. We'd lay them down that way to fill the whole roadbed, sometimes for long stretches. Those stone made crevasses that the water followed until it made sense to channel it away."

Wow...I'd call that Yankee ingenuity as its very best! Those old guys drained some places that would otherwise be mud season nightmares and, as hard as it is to believe, helped the farmers out to boot. Those farmers were glad to get modern fences—all except one farmer. Today I was out in the woods finishing up the tree tapping and tore my brand-new rubber boot on a strand of ancient barbed wire; I'd love to have the stone walls back!

Chapter 50

Flatchucks Forever

WE HAVE TWO TYPES OF PEOPLE in Vermont these days, the Flatlanders and the Woodchucks. Anyone who has moved in within the last thirty years is a Flatlander, regardless of point of origin—Colorado, the Pocanos, Switzerland—they're all Flatlanders. Flatlanders are generally distinguishable by three qualities: they're left-leaning, have a questioning nature, and show a propensity toward outdoor recreation. Woodchucks are long-term Vermonters. Most of them are right-leaning, have an accepting nature even when it kills them, and spend much of their off time splitting wood. Flatlanders and Woodchucks get along with each other just fine 'cause, to use an old Vermont term, there ain't no percentage in fightin'. There are fewer Woodchucks than ever these days but those left are still sweet—sweet as the maple syrup that will forever course their veins.

There used to be two distinct Woodchuck dialects but because of the mobility of late, the peaks and valleys of Vermont dialect have, dare I say, flattened out. Two of my three most memorable sugarhouse visitors this season were Woodchucks. The third was a Flatlander. Woodchuck talk comes in two speeds, fast and slow, which reminds me of the symbols on my tractor's accelerator, the rabbit and the turtle.

The other day a "rabbit" visited. He was a stout young man with dark, curly hair that squeezed out of a stained John Deere cap. He came on like a bulldozer in the sugarbush, his eyes aiming immediately at my wood-chip burner.

"You boil wiff wood chips I useta run one a them rigs them rigs boil sap like a sumbitch haw haw yes-sir been sugarin' all my life grew up in Eden but now live down ta Dummerston in southern Vermont still boilin' sap but only on a small rig got 'bout two hundred buckets hung sap ain't runnin' much this year—say, hear they're messin' with the syrup gradin' law down ta the legislature in Montpelier they don't know nothin' up there on the Hill anyway well better get on back to the Banana Belt ha ha nice meetin' you keep boilin' wiff them wood chips they'll boil like a sumbitch."

With that he about-faced and headed out the sugarhouse door. He returned three times with second thoughts, however, before his tired-looking wife finally coaxed him into the car and down the road toward the Banana Belt.

The day the "turtle" visited I was feeling a little bored and anxious for some company. All of a sudden company arrived in the form of a wrinkled up old man who I recognized as someone my father used to know from the hills of Elmore, Vermont. He hobbled in, led by a handmade cane. Before he spoke, he took a huge breath of sugarhouse air:

"Know Harry," he said.

"Oh," I replied, "I'm Harry, Jr. They call me Burr. Did you go to school with my father?"

"Nope."

"Oh, well I remember you Mr. Simpson—haven't seen you for ages. I believe you come from up Elmore way."

"Yup."

"You used to milk Jersey cows up there, didn't you?"

"Yup."

"Did you know that Harry passed away back in '99?" I said.

"You don't say," he said as he slowly turned to leave. His greatest eloquence, however, came with a single tear that ran down his face like a drop of sap.

My third visitor, the Flatlander, is a great friend who used to make maple syrup at the foot of Hunger Mountain. He was a good sugarmaker and the one who got me started with wood chips some fourteen years ago—taught me a lot, he did. He came in the sugarhouse full of compliments about some of my accomplishments as a businessman and a book author. I stopped him short, however, and reminded him that I'm just a Woodchuck.

"Well," Lou said, "I'd rather think you're more of a Woodcharles."

I thought about what he had said and, although it immediately struck me as funny, the aftertaste planted a seed of concern. You see, there are no class distinctions here in Vermont. We all work together and help each other out. Sure, there are different ways of talkin' and leanin' but, just like the different grades of maple syrup, that's what makes life interesting. The short of it is quite simple—we're all Vermonters. 'Nough said!

Chapter 51

Mason Dixon Magic

TWO YEARS AGO I TOOK an unorthodox vacation to points west in search of Vermont sugar weather. Maple sugarmakers thrive on springtime freezing nights and thawing days which we normally inherit from the west. That year we were in the throes of an obstinate and frigid early March. A trek over the Mississippi River and a few right-hand turns led me to the farm of Dale and Karen Green in Castalia, Iowa. There, besides finding a perfect American farm couple, I also found the freezing nights and thawing days I sought. They had 2,200 trees tapped (yes, believe it or not, in Iowa) and sap was a drippin'. After a wonderful meal of Karin's hot corn bread and homemade soup, I beckoned that weather to follow me back to Vermont. It did and we wound up having a fair sugar season.

This year our January sits thumbing its nose at Morse Farm's cross-country skiers who have all but given up on any lasting and ski-able snow. Being somewhat hooked on unorthodox vacations, I just returned from the Midwest again. I invited a neighbor, Tim Carver, to accompany me this time. Our wives seemed glad to be rid of us for a week and we headed out January 3. We drove toward America's heartland and the huge snowfalls that we'd been hearing about in the news, quickly chalking off miles with talk of politics, farming and fixin' machinery. As we approached the Mississippi River, the huge blue skies and green countryside that lay ahead offered a complete absence of winter's snowy face that we sought. Our thoughts turned toward personalities more of the human kind.

A quick phone call and a southerly change in direction led us to Dyersburg, Tennessee, the home of Mr. Earl Hinkel. Earl has been on my e-mail list for a couple of years and, judging by his consistent wise and witty comments, stood out as a man whose hand I'd like to shake. We planned on spending a few minutes with Earl and then traveling on, a concept we would soon find totally disallowed by southern hospitality. He met us at Dyersburg's Best Western where he had reserved a room for us.

"Burr Morse," he said. "I'm honored that you would drive all the way to Dyersburg to see me!"

The man who grasped my hand and then pulled me into a smothering bear hug looked thin and in good shape. His face only hinted of old age. We soon learned that this youthful eighty-seven year old would capture our hearts for two days, wining, dining, and showing us the sights of western Tennessee. After a most delicious steak dinner with Earl and his son and daughter-in-law at their favorite restaurant, we were taken to their home. The Hinkels' rambling house nestles in a hilly, oaken setting. Earl has an immaculate apartment at one end filled with classy furnishings and models of trains, airplanes, and action toys—in Earl's words: "I've spent my life fascinated with trains, planes, and Janes—now I'm down to just trains and planes!" He lives there with his best friend, Mr. Rebel Hinkel, a huge beagle with a beaming southern personality but a physique that more resembles a manatee (in spite of the two-mile forced march Earl takes him on, two times a day).

Our second day began with a visit to a local icon, Mr. Red Bond. On the edge of Dyersburg, we turned right and down a long, twisting lane to a rustic homestead. Miscellaneous auto parts, wood leavings, and rusting farm machinery sat close to the remains of a thriving tomato patch. The yard had the obvious markings of a jack-of-all-trades. Before we went in, Earl opened his trunk and withdrew a supermarket pastry box—"Can't visit Red without doughnuts," he said. We entered one of the outbuildings without knocking, and walked through a room that held a whole century's collection of nickknacks and antique furniture in various stages of repair. A booming "C'mon in" beckoned us to a room at the back where sat a huge, bald man with a smile as broad as a honeysuckle blossom. After we shook Red Bond's hand, we sat around a square table and opened the donuts. Within five minutes, Red had both announced that "his great grand daddy" had been captured two times by the Yankees and asked if I was a Methodist. My affirmative answer opened the door to two hours of Red's stories, some gently off-color, and several handmade gifts from his woodworking shop. As we left, I promised to send Red a chunk of sugar maple to turn on his lathe. In return I had received enough Red Bond stories to fill a future column.

Earl showed us the sights of downtown Dyersburg, including the drugstore where he still holds a five-day-a-week job, and multiple churches. We were impressed by the size and obvious vitality of those southern churches, comparing it to organized religion's diminishing presence back home. That same day we drove to Reelfoot Lake, a 13,000-acre natural wonder. It was caused back in the 1800s by a giant earthquake that caused the Mississippi River to flow backward. Reelfoot Lake offered views of bald eagles perched on cypress trees and a nearby catfish restaurant, which is about as unique to two Vermont boys as views of bald eagles.

Before we left Earl's place on the last day, I opened my car's trunk and ceremonially swept in a bunch of southern hospitality to bring back to Vermont. We said our goodbyes, and Tim Carver and I headed back east. As I sit here today finishing this column, snow is falling and there's a spirit in the air that has been lacking all winter so far—guess that southern hospitality Earl sent home with me did the trick for the time being!

Chapter 52

Pocket Pain

I'VE RECENTLY BEEN WORKING in the sugar woods with my friend, Allen Jacobs. One thing about my work this time of year is that the woods are quiet, and although our hands are busy with the preparation of miles of plastic tubing for the oncoming sugar season, our mouths are free to shoot the breeze. One of our last talks, in fact, was on the subject of miles—vacation miles. I had just returned from a week's vacation to a snowy world of hard labor and my back was killin' me; I allowed to Allen, semi-tongue-in-cheek, that vacations are designed to get folks in trouble and that a smart person would simply never go away. He told of just such a person.

It seems Maurice Page, a cooper by trade from over in Corinth, never left the state of Vermont. One day a flatlander asked him why. Maurice deliberately put down the tool he was working with, looked out the shop window at the bucolic countryside, and simply replied, "No need."

Wow...think of all the trouble it would save if we all took a page from Maurice's book! The trouble on my last trip started somewhere between Chicago and Manchester, New Hampshire, in seat 13A on United Airlines Flight 4720. The first hint came with a dull ache in my left buttock, right where my wallet sat in my back pocket. "Hmmm," I thought,"never felt quite that way before." I was already a little tense, being an infrequent flyer on a very bumpy flight, in aisle 13! The turbulence stayed active right to the end and when we finally came in for a landing at Manchester Airport that Boeing 737 bounced around like, as my father would have said, "a fart in a hot skillet."

The next day, for the first time in my life, my back was so bad that walking and sitting were excruciating...going to work in the sugar woods was unthinkable. My good wife, Betsy, had started the near impossible search for a chiropractor who would take on a new patient at the spur of the moment when Allen, my sugar woods helper, came in the door.

"Dr. Jimmy over in Williamstown is the guy for you," he said as he reached for our phone. "Jimmy'll help you and I guarantee he'll take you in today."

Sure enough, Allen had me an appointment in the time it would take to crunch a bone, and Betsy and I headed for Williamstown to the office of Dr. James Garand. As Betsy drove, I thought of another time I visited Williamstown.

I had bought a wrecked GMC pickup, sight unseen. It was drivable but badly misshapen and humped up like a constipated old hound. I limped her into Williamstown to the body shop of a guy who had a biblical reputation for straightening truck and car frames. He came out into the yard and dropped to his knees for a closer look. I worried that he'd recommend automotive last rites and a good scrapyard but he finally he spoke: "The cuss is a little swayback but I believe I can put her back on the road." I left it with him and, sure enough, he straightened it into one of the best pickups I ever had...drove it for years, I did.

Dr. Jimmy's office is in the basement of his home, only a country mile from that famous body shop. I crab-walked in to his reception area and found him on the phone with a patient. I would learn that he was a one-man show; he answered his own phone, made his own appointments, did his own billing, and was not opposed to trading part of his services for maple syrup. He glanced at me while still on the phone, no doubt thinking, "The cuss is a little swayback" and over the course of three more visits, sure enough, he "put me back on the road".

He said that my femoral nerve was the problem and didn't disagree with my suspicions that vacation miles played into the cause. It was my first experience with his kind of doctor and I'll never forget the wracking and cracking that made me feel a little better after every visit. He also used, like Maurice Page the cooper, Vermont wisdom when he spoke. "Work smarter...Let your machines do what your back isn't meant to do...Be willing to change your ways," he said. I'm willing to take his advice but probably won't heed Mr. Page's words on taking vacations; as perfect as Vermont is, the next time I feel the urge to go away, I'll probably go for a spell and then come home. One thing for sure, however—wherever life takes me, I'll always obey Dr. Jimmy's final words to me: "Don't ever carry your wallet in your back pocket!"

Chapter 53

Possum Possibilities

THINGS ARE STARTING TO GREEN up here in Vermont in spite of a chilly, rainy post-sugar season. We've finally gotten the fences fixed and today a stock trailer backed up to our acreage out front. A guy got out, critically scanned the electric fence, and lowered the trailer's tailgate. Inside, a small herd of mixed bovines stood, dirty from winter stalls and confused about their future. With a little prodding, they slowly sniffed their way down the tailgate and onto the green grass. The cow guy and I watched, knowing contact with the grass would trigger a ritual of spring I love to watch. Sure enough, those critters didn't let me down. They blatted and bellowed and kicked their hooves high, drunk for a short time with freedom. We watched until they settled down and began a summer of grazing. The cow guy and I shook hands and he drove off, down the road, beyond the land that my ancestors had cleared for cows.

We sold our herd years ago. This place stayed cowless for one season which about drove me crazy. All summer long I sensed unrest from those ancestors who shouted from every ragged clump, "Graze this land!" I knew I needed to honor them for their hard work so long ago. They cleared the best of Vermont for the cows and the worst of it for the sheep. My old friend, Ernest Gould, used to say, "The devil's apron strings broke over Vermont." He meant, of course, that we can thank the devil for the rocks and boulders that curse these Vermont hills and valleys—hellish for man, but pure paradise for sheep. Our sheep industry thrived for a long time. It built our villages and fortified our economy; then that same economy, fickle like the weather in Vermont, took the sheep away.

One day back during sugaring, a couple from New Zealand visited our sugarhouse. I welcomed them, recognizing their accent early in our conversation. They were fascinated by the maple process, literally a world detached from their sheep and cattle back home. One thing led to another and before long we were talking about New Zealand's thriving sheep industry. Being farm people, they were full of facts and figures. We were, in fact, feeling quite satisfied with our little "cultural exchange" when I said something stupid: I said I had no use for wool because it's so itchy and heavy. The woman looked at me as though I had just doused her with hot maple syrup—I sensed a sticky situation ahead. She reached into her trousers, stretched a six-inch section of her undergarment toward me and said in her stern New Zealand voice: "Wool's neither itchy nor heavy—feel it, mate." I looked at her husband, speaking of "mates," before I considered feeling his wife's underpants. He smiled with that "you'd better do what she says" sort of look. I slowly reached out and felt the softest, silkiest fabric that ever snuggled an ample set of hips. I wanted a pair for myself.

She said it was made from choice merino wool and, are you ready for this, roadkill 'possum. That's right, 'possum fur. "There's a right devilish population of the varmits back home," she said," and they offer a bounty to those who bring them in, roadkill or otherwise. They put 'em through a chicken plucker and weave their fur into this wool." She offered a touch to everyone else in the sugarhouse before she tucked herself back in.

I've since thought a lot about that nice couple and our little exchange. It seems absurd that we've lost our Vermont sheep industry, especially now that I know how versatile wool is. In fact, I'm thinking of introducing a new product line to these parts: It's to be called "'Possum-in-Your-Pants" undergarments. I'll be looking for 6,000 Vermont farmers wanting to put their land back into viable, lucrative production. We'll be starting up small woolen mills in places like North Montpelier and Bridgewater and hiring labor at a fair rate. We'll bring back the grain mills, livestock sales, and country markets. Vermont hillsides will be white year-round with snow in winter, sheep in summer. Oh, and we'll need an inexpensive source of 'possum fur from points south—tons and tons of it. Any takers out there?

Chapter 54

Reflections on Sugarin'

I GUESS IT'S MY HEREDITY that led me to the sap bucket the other day—that and a need for a good drink of sap. The bucket hung on a gnarly old maple with two others placed randomly around the tree. It was one of those days when the sap was ticking off at about 120 drops per minute and I could see as I approached that the bucket was full and running over. I slid off the cover, careful not to spill anymore than I had to, and peered into the clear liquid. To my astonishment I saw in the reflection, not a weathered fifty-eight year old but a round faced boy of twelve. The boy's face moved gently with the liquid's rippling and memories came fast, like the sap flow, and almost real.

It was the seventh grade and I had a science project to do. I had always been curious about whether other species of hardwood trees had usable sap. It was the spring of the year, the time when sap flowed from the 3,000 sugar maples that my family tapped at the time. I knew of a few spare buckets and there were trees of different species within walking distance of my house. The teacher thought it was a good idea and helped me prepare for the project in a scientific way. After getting my father's okay, I headed out one day, armed with the tree tapper and enough supplies to tap a beech, yellow birch, ash, and elm. I remember leaving the woods that day feeling on the edge of an important scientific breakthrough. The following days, however, proved disappointing. As the surrounding maples ran flush with sap, the buckets on the non-maples stood barren day after day. I was about to give up on the experiment when one day I slid the lid off the elm's bucket and—voilà—there in the bottom was a bubbly, puckery mass. It was hideous but scientific results nevertheless!

I pulled the bucket from the tree and ran to the house. "I've got sap from an elm tree," I shouted, as I burst in to show my mother. She was impressed in a guarded sort of way. She refused my offer of a taste, something I had not brought myself to do either—the stuff was disgusting! Next, I ran down the road to my grandparents' house. My Grandma Morse was very impressed and even dipped her pinky in. About the time she put it to her lips for a taste, my older siblings came to the door but backed off when they saw what was happening. They acted quite subdued and when Grandma Morse announced my find and invited them to taste they melted into the background. Grandma, although repulsed by the taste and texture, was praising of my efforts and suggested I follow through with some laboratory testing. I remember wondering, as I walked home, why she seemed to be my only true ally.

I think it was my mother who finally owned up. It seems my siblings had spied on my operation from the start and decided to help nature a bit. They had mixed small amounts of everything from the kitchen cupboard with something I won't even mention from another room in the house, stirred it into a slurry, and planted it in the elm tree bucket—I had been duped! As I remember, my older siblings threatened me with death if Grandma Morse ever found out what she had tasted and I went on to figure out a quick, alternate science project. In all the forty-six years since then, I've never tapped anything but a maple.

It's not unusual for kids up in this neck of the woods to go out in the spring of the year and tap a few maples. After all, the trees are there and a bucket brimming with sap brings great satisfaction. The grueling job of gathering and boiling, however, quickly trumps the satisfaction for most kids. There's a kid who lives down the road from our farm who is different, though. He lives across from a grove of young maples and about four years ago he tapped one large tree and hung a couple of milk jugs. I thought it was cute but expected to see a diminished interest as the season went on. The next year, however, he expanded his operation to two more trees and a half dozen the third year. This spring, he has proved his mettle as "sugarmaker for life," at least to this lifetime sugarmaker—white milk jugs hang like giant puff balls as far as the eye can see on that hillside of maples. In fact, we have many tourists who drive past his place on the way to our farm. They all mention the milk jugs hanging on the hillside and want to know if it's a legitimate venture. "Why yes," I say. "The boy has maple in his blood and is in training for a lifetime of sugarin'. He'll never get it out of his system—you can't get any more legit than that!"

I just returned from our sugarhouse, lame and weary. That huge sap run is still going on. My son Tommy has been bringing in load after load in his sap wagon and I've been burning the candle at both ends boiling it.

Although I love sugarin', I get really tired standing at our big, stainless steel evaporator watching the levels of boiling sap and drawing off batches of syrup. Today something led my eyes to the upper part of the sugarhouse where the evaporator stands tall in layers of preheaters and piggyback pans. I saw my reflection in the stainless mass but this time it was of a white-bearded fifty-eight year old who looks weathered and older than his years. At that moment I considered the time when I would no longer be able to sugar—old sugarmakers sweetly fade away, you know. When that time comes, I'm thankful there's folks to carry on, like Tommy and his sap wagon, and that kid down the road with maple in his blood.

Chapter 55

Sap Tanknology

I'M WRITING THIS FROM Kansas City the day before my return flight home. This year's late-winter vacation has included a 2,000-mile drive out to Albuquerque, up into Colorado and then back through the Nebraska plains to Kansas City...wonderful time! My memory tank is full of potential stories of this trip but, speaking of full tanks, I'm thinking of my return to pre-sugarin' Vermont. Sometimes I compare modern-day sugarin' to the computer age because of all the changes we're making but we'll never change one thing: dealing with huge amounts of liquids requires huge tanks.

Just like most sugarmakers these days, we're updating our process to include vacuum-filled tubing lines but I'm leaving the higher plumbing up to my son Tommy and he sure is reveling in the cause. Right now he's got enough combinations of piping, glass spheres, and steam valves to make a Tennessee hillbilly slap his knees. At the end of his rigging is the prettiest stainless steel tank you ever saw.

Tommy's new tank sits at the southernmost border of our farm, down off Center Road. All the sap from the sugar woods above it flows to that tank which sits on a rugged plank frame. He built the frame on piers sunk into the ground to ensure it stays solid and level. The tank sits in a welded steel cradle, strong enough to hold its volume of 1,500 gallons. On top of it is a cover he fabricated with truss rafters and handsome, red roofing. It's a setup that will be easier to clean and service and, as my father would have said, "Ain't bad to look at either."

When I was young, ancient wood-stave sap tanks had given way to newer, galvanized models. Sometimes back then we even improvised; no matter what it was made of, if it was patchable for water retention, it would work for sap. Come to think of it, my father's increased gum chewing during sugar season sometimes had purpose beyond exercising his jawbone! I had an experience once in sap tanknology that almost proved me too slow to chew gum and ride a sap wagon at the same time. It also became the highlight of my sugar season.

We had an old iron tank that was totally enclosed except for a small porthole in the top. We used it on the Chevy farm truck for hauling sap from distant maple groves. One day, I noticed it was rustier than it should be inside and knew the evaporator company sold a paint they billed as "approved for use on sap tanks." I manipulated the tank into the basement of our sugar shack with block and tackle, crawled in the porthole, and went at the interior with sandpaper. Every once in a while I'd poke my head out the porthole for a gulp of fresh air but I generally disregarded the matter of air quality. The next day, after the dust settled, I crawled back in and started painting.

It felt good, I thought, to be taking care of that piece of farm maintenance. The more I painted, the better it felt. Soon, my mind started to philosophize about the wonderment of old sap tanks and life in general. I even found myself singing "Oh What a Beautiful Morning" at the top of my rust-blackened lungs. Thankfully the singing alerted my father who suddenly appeared, peering through the porthole into my sky-high world of paint fumes! Dad coaxed me out into the fresh air and walked me around, explaining the stupidity of what I had just done. Needless to say, I've since approached my painting jobs with more common sense and soberness of mind.

Often these days, folks pine for old sugarin' times when wood fires crackled and sap buckets filled with a rhythmic ping, ping, ping. Sometimes I miss the old days myself but it's fun, at the same time, to see the modern generation take over. Yup, change is always good and sometimes even smarter and better lookin'. These days nobody ever paints sap tanks and, although plastic ones work, the smartest modern sugarmaker buys his tanks of the stainless steel variety. Soon Tommy's new tank will be filling up with spring's most famous nectar and every time we pump from it, we'll anticipate sweet rewards and appreciate the merits of modern tanknology.

Chapter 56

Grandpa's Skyhook

DO YOU BELIEVE IN SKYHOOKS? My Grandpa Morse sure did. They were especially handy when we were putting away farm equipment for the winter. He taught me so much about levers, block and tackle, and not "busting my gut." But when we really got stumped on how to get something back to the far recesses of the storage shed, Grandpa'd call for the skyhooks. He always said those magic words with a wink and, by golly, the problem at hand always magically fell into place right then and there; skyhooks, they were—I never saw them but if Grandpa believed in them, that was good enough for me. I gave up on Santa Claus and the Easter Bunny early on: a big bag of wind in red clothing and a rabbit that lays eggs? —c'mom, give me a break! Skyhooks, on the other hand, were real and essential for me well into my teens. Grandpa died back in 1975 but to this day I occasionally search the heavens for aid from one of his wonderful devices.

Recently a couple of events have made me think of skyhooks; both relate to the huge dumping of snow we got on Saint Valentine's Day. The first one happened about midnight on the fourteenth. The snow was coming down so hard by mid-morning that I kept my tractor going all day long plowing our yard. I quit at suppertime, exhausted and thinking the snow would soon stop. Around midnight I was aroused from a deep sleep by the alarm system down at our store. I sleepily pulled on my multi-layers to the whoop, whoop, whooping of the siren that sounds loud and clear in my bedroom. When I exited my house, I was amazed to find the huge accumulation that had fallen since I had hit the sack—it hadn't stopped. I wallowed, painfully, out my walk and down the driveway to my tractor in the lower barn. It started easily, hardly cool from its day of labor. I put it into a low gear and crept down the roadway that circles our store.

Our alarm system is hooked up to the state police but I knew those folks would be pre-occupied by the storm and might not be able to respond quickly. I had also been told to never enter my building if I suspected there was a thief at work inside. The scene was surreal, the falling snow in the middle of the night—I was glad to hold my hero instinct at bay. The tractor labored as it approached the store, its footprints sunken a full twelve inches in fluffy snow. Suddenly it occurred to me that for a thief to have entered my building, his boots would have left a deep furrow from the road to his entry point—that is if he wasn't lowered by skyhooks! I kept my eyes peeled for that furrow as the tractor slowly completed its circle and saw none. I stopped the machine at the front door but before I got off and approached, I lifted my eyes toward heaven, beseeching Grandpa Morse:

"You sure?" I asked.

"I'm sure," he said. "Skyhooks only work for good people."

I went in and found all was well, except for a cardboard sign that had fallen, like a dry leaf, in front of the offending motion detector.

The other event happened in broad daylight the next day, in our sugar woods. I was out in the Valentine's dumping with my snowshoes on, working on our maple tubing. Each grueling step sank deeply into the soft snow but the pressure of our oncoming sugar season kept me plodding. All of a sudden, I dropped up to my middle into a depression that had been camouflaged by drifted snow. My snowshoes, anchored by the snow and miscellaneous deadfall, held me like I was in a leg-hold trap. I had just started pondering my options when my cell phone rang.

"How ya doin' Harry—it's Salvatore from Imaginative Ideas." (I knew he was trying to sell me something because he used my real name, Harry.) "Say—we're makin' a new plastic phone book cover. We wantcha ta be on it."

"No thanks," I said, quickly hanging up the phone—"Imaginative ideas, plastic phone book covers, indeed!" I scoffed and then I had a second thought; I needed an imaginative idea and his mention of "plastic" reminded me of a coil of plastic tubing I used for repairs that hung from my middle—thank you Salvatore! I looked up, beseeching Grandpa once again, and there overhead, was a stout maple limb. I uncoiled the tubing and tossed it with the skill of Roy Rogers over the limb, grabbed both ends, and pulled myself back to snowy terra firma. After brushing the snow off and making sure my legs worked okay, I looked heavenward again and thanked Grandpa Morse for the most wonderful tool of all, his magical skyhook.

Chapter 57

The Sound of Snow

IN ONE OF MY RECENT WRITINGS, I mentioned "the gentle sound of snow falling and the scraping sounds of snowplows." Since 'tis that season, I do have some thoughts on both subjects. I was called on the former by one of my readers, Gayle. Gayle chided me: "Now, Burr, I've always been told that snow falls soundlessly." She did, however, add the disclaimer that she is a native of California's Central Valley, where it rarely snows. I thrive on input from my readers like the Vermont countryside thrives on three feet of snow, and feel compelled to answer this question once and for all. To do that I'll draw from the depths of my Vermont being, breathe deep, and put myself outside on a January night at the beginning of a blizzard.

It always begins with the sound of a freight train six miles away down at Montpelier Junction. The horn starts softly, like a lullaby, but crescendos as the train nears the Junction. A long wail gives way to the sound of a huge diesel motor, straining all the way to Middlesex. Then it's gone. Trains only sound off like that when the atmosphere has a pre-storm edge to it and on this otherwise still night, I wait for the snow to begin. The weatherman agrees with the train—his forecasted blizzard starts around 6 p.m.. I go out into the yard and stand like a zombie. Feathery whiteness coats me like the softest down and I know there'll be another inch in ten minutes; that's when the snow makes a sound. It's not loud—think of it as a babbling brook with the volume turned way down, a trillion feathers falling from the sky, or just a gentle change in the stillness; but to a Vermonter it's clear— the sound of falling snow.

Most folks dig in while the blizzard is going on but after it ends and the stillness returns, they begin to dig out. The sound of digging out varies from the whirring of snow blowers to the clomping of snow shovels. I favor the rumbling, scraping sounds of the huge, winged trucks that run the roads. Their motors roar between ten changing gears and the guy inside must be a genius —how else could he keep that thing upright, on task and accident free? These days that guy has special training, a special license, and lots of liability. When I was a boy, the plow guy was much more relaxed.

Our plow guy was old Eddy, the road commissioner of Calais. He was a tall man with a broad smile that featured one gold tooth right in front. There was no storm too big for the huge town bulldozer decked out for winter with a V-plow and two hydraulic wings. The wings were for pushing snow back further on the open roads. Eddy knew the wing control levers like the back of his hands, hands that also knew the contours of a liquor bottle. Back then, things were slower, including the traffic, and as long as Eddy got the job done, no one cared that he was usually drinkin'!

My friend, Edna Armstrong, told of one time Eddy got confused—said it was probably the wrong combination of snow and alcohol that day! Her husband, Arthur, was in their living room up off George Road when Eddy went past with the plow rig. Arthur said he was plowing pretty straight, but had the wings in the up position when they should have been down. When he got into the valley where the brook crosses, Eddy lowered the wings just as he got to the bridge. "That old machine swept the entire bridge railing system off into the brook like so many bowling pins," Arthur said. "Once he cleared the bridge, Eddy raised the wings and continued on his way, not knowing anything was wrong!"

I can still hear in my mind the clickity-clack of that old Calais bull-dozer. It's gone now, as is Eddy, the plow guy. These days we have different sounds for a faster pace. The guardrails and mailboxes still take a winter beating (we know from haste rather than inebriation), but the bustle of snow removal still has a personality of its own. The one thing that has not changed, however, is the sound of falling snow—yup, it's true. If you're a Vermonter, go out and stand still the night before one of those diggin' out days. You'll hear it.

Chapter 58

Sweet and Sour Journey

I WAS HONORED RECENTLY to be the keynote speaker at an Ontario Maple Producers banquet. The banquet was the culmination of a three-day convention on St. Joseph Island, Ontario, an island just north of Sault Ste. Marie, Michigan. Being a Vermont sugarmaker and typically snobbish about "Vermont maple," accepting a maple haven invitation that far west was a hard pill to swallow but St. Joseph Island proved to be a wonderful experience. Its distance from Vermont seemed to be no problem at all maple-wise, but logistically...well, let's just say this Vermonter doesn't do very well on airplanes.

My brother Elliott and I reported to the airport in Burlington an hour early for our 6:30 a.m. flight to Newark that led to Detroit, that led to Alpena, that led to Chippewa, somewhere south of the Arctic Circle. I was a little uptight about the potential scrutiny of the metal and plastic maple props in my carry-on bag, but ironically the water bottle Betsy had sent with me became the problem. "No liquids," the security guy said and his next statement, "either drink it or dump it," was an immediate affront to this cheap old Vermonter who can't throw anything away. I glugged it. Once airborne I braced myself for the trip and accepted the liberal offering of drinks, something airlines, for some odd reason, consider as important to the concept of flight as wings. Our stopover in Newark was short and left no room for the bathroom, so as we approached the gate in Detroit, I suddenly realized that my last Diet Pepsi had put me over the edge. "I can wait though," I thought as the stewardess announced that we were to stay in our seats with belts fastened. Then the pilot came on and said that our gate was occupied and we would have to wait for ten minutes.

About half way through the second ten minutes, I knew I would lose the battle. I unfastened my seat belt, got up, and turned to face the back of the plane. For some reason everything went into slow motion, like something huge was about to happen in my life. Our stewardess sat behind an orange tape stretched across the aisle with her arms crossed, seemingly daring any of us to try using the lavatory. As I headed in her direction, she mouthed the words, "Sit down!" punctuated with a stiff pointed finger. By then I was doing a little dance, bent slightly at the waist with my knees crossed. I mouthed the words "I gotta pee!" and pointed to my problem area. Again, she mouthed those words, this time with venom. Our sweet, smiling stewardess had transformed into the Incredible Hulk and she started to assume a fighting crouch. All of a sudden adrenalin surged with that other liquid that was by now up to my eyeballs. She and I met, nose to nose, she the protector of people who fly, I the poster child for everyone with a bladder. I was....well...pissed.

"How dare you say I can't relieve myself!"

"Sit down!"

"If you don't let me in that bathroom I'm going to pee my pants right here, and..." signing and sealing the last word, "...it ain't going to be pretty!"

She indignantly said she would call the captain and have the plane stopped. As I rushed the bathroom door and began exercising my right, I felt the huge plane with 180 people aboard grind to a stop. The relief was wonderful and any temptation to feel the power of what I had just done went down the drain along with the adrenalin. I returned to my seat like a dog with its tail between its legs. The plane started up for a few seconds and stopped; we had been within ten feet of our gate when my crisis occurred! When we exited the plane, the stewardess was standing at the door, back to her smiling self. I smiled back; my bladder had forgiven her for her total lack of understanding.

The rest of our flight proved non-eventful and we were met at the Chippewa Airport by Mr. Arden Irwin, a St. Joseph Island maple guy who earned his right to retire as a sugarmaker by working forty years in the steel mills of Sault Ste. Marie (referred to by all Ontarioites as "The Soo"). Arden drove us through a friendly Canadian Customs and on through the flat, Ontario countryside. St. Joseph Island greeted us with a certain maple magic the minute a short bridge delivered us to its shores. The island centers around the villages of Richards Landing and Hilton. On the roads that connect the villages, maple signs announce family sugar camps, Biggers, Thompsons, Gilbertsons and many others among the island's 2,000 residents. During the three-day convention, we visited multi sugar camps, most of which employ plastic tubing, vacuum, and expertise to make sap water flow from point A to point B on flat land!

We learned a lot that weekend about changes emerging in the modern world of maple sugarmaking; some of those things will make our job more difficult in the future. Sugarmakers, however, will always rise to the occasion. In my address I acknowledged the big job maple sugarmaking is and played down Vermont's own image in favor of our international maple area of America and Canada. "Maple diplomacy is key," I said, "and we need to learn the difference between problems with a capital P and minor annoyances." All the time I was thinking of that stewardess and her airline.

Chapter 59

Sugarin' Near and Far

THE DAY STARTED OUT DARK and ominous. I was boiling from a monstrous sap run the day before and rain was falling in torrents. There were several places in the old metal roof where rain found its way in through the same holes that exposed the gray sky over central Vermont. Before I went to work, I had read an e-mail from my friend, Mac, who winters in Florida. It started off ominous, like the weather: "I just went and had a snort," he said. Poor man, I thought, recalling my grandfather Morse who used to feel imprisoned this time of year in Florida. He'd take his splitting hammer and wedge and in the spring, when sugar season pangs came gushing, he'd split all the wood he could find in the neighborhood, starting with the live oak, and ending with the palm trees. Mac's e-mail went on: "Theresa is gone so I went to the jug and had a good pull." Poor, poor Mac, I thought, wishing he could be back home in Vermont enjoying the therapy of my sugarhouse.

Such sugar season passion commonly affects Vermonters, both absentee and in the flesh, but there's magic in that thar steam even for flatlanders. I received a call back in mid-February from a guy in Savannah, Georgia.

"Ah wonder if you could fullfill a lahf -long dream for me," he said. "When ah was a chauld ah read a thang called 'Weekly Readah' and it talked about maple sugarin' in VERmont and ah've always wanted t'see it."

I said I'd be glad to show him sugarin', told him when he should arrive, and that my brother, Elliott, would pick him up when his train got in. I was boiling up a mighty steam the day he and Elliott walked into the sugarhouse. Joe Colson, a big man, came right up to the evaporator, offered a huge hand, and took the same size whiff.

"Ah'll teh you what," he said (he started most every sentence by telling me what) "Ah 'preciate so much what you've done for me." I told him that I was just reciprocating a thing called southern hospitality and beckoned to a stool close to where I stood boiling. We chatted about the maple process and then went on to some light banter about each other's state. I pointed to the sea of ruts just outside our sugarhouse and said we Vermonters are righteous about mud, our state soil. He told about a woman who referred to Vermont as "the big muddy," and then topped my homeland putdown with one of his own. "Ah'll teh you what...Georgia is the most civilahzed state in the south today...we mostly all wearin' shoes in the summah!" When he left, he said his maple vacation was "better than a trip to Europe." Joe Colson was, indeed, a great southern gentleman and my life was made much richer by reciprocating his region's famous hospitality.

Another memorable sugarhouse visitor was a Vermont man. Age had diminished his stride to a feeble shuffling. He came across the sugarhouse, seemingly led by a white, ceramic mug. He shuffled up to where I was boiling and, without words, offered the mug to me. Both being Vermonters with sugarhouse roots, neither of us needed words; he was asking me to fill his mug with sweet sap from the front pan. I took it, scooped into the steaming liquid with my dipper, and filled it to the top. I handed it back to him, offering no words of warning. He knew how hot it was. He put it to his lips and sipped as though his life depended on it...and it probably did. You see, for some elderly Vermonters, living till maple sugar season and drinking sweetness from the front pan strengthens their spirit and prepares them for another year. He asked for another cupful before he left and, as he shuffled away, he spoke for the first time: "Much obliged," he said.

Maple season, indeed, brings magic. Its magic travels a road called nostalgia and may knock at doors all over the world or simply stay t'home in a steamy sugarhouse. It always involves wonderful smells and sweet sips, and like my friend, Mac, requires an occasional "pullin'" from the syrup jug.

Chapter 60

Truth in Silence

A WHILE BACK I ATTENDED the Vermont Maple Festival up in St. Albans. The bright sky promised a banner day as I headed toward Vermont's northwest corner. Just north of Burlington, where the beautiful Adirondacks rise up from Lake Champlain's western shore, I was reminded of the sprinkling of maple forests that stretch all the way to Wisconsin. To the north lay the maple vastness of Quebec. I knew that people from all maple regions would be represented at the festival. I also knew none would be more prominent than those whose maple clout has sweetened the Vermont Maple Festival for forty years now— the Franklin County sugarmakers.

Franklin County, the heart and soul of Vermont sugarmaking, has gushed maple sap as long as Vermont has been Vermont. The Franklin County muscle gushing, however, comes from Fairfield just over a steep hill and across a broad swamp to the east of St. Albans. In spite of its swampy introduction, springtime Fairfield is a snowy, steamy patchwork of rolling pastures, pristine homesteads, and sugarhouses on every hillside. It's the sugaringist gosh-darned place in the whole universe and you might wonder why? The short answer is simple—it's got more trees to make more sap— but short, simple answers are not always popular in Fairfield, Vermont. What's most popular in Fairfield, in fact, are no answers at all.

Years of maple dominance have given Fairfield sugarmakers an independence unequaled anywhere and I certainly don't say that disparagingly— Fairfield sugarmakers are extremely likable, will take the shirts off their backs to help anyone, are hard working, and, oh, they're as honest as their syrup is pure. They practice their honesty, however, with a caveat as gnarly as a 200-year-old maple: there are certain questions they simply won't answer. Yesterday I ran into a grandfather Fairfield sugarmaker whom I recognized as owner of a large dairy farm and maple operation. (Before I proceed I must explain the Fairfield Dodge: first they hesitate, take a huge draw of air, cradle their chin with their right thumb and forefinger so it scrunches their face into an unrecognizable mass, and then mutter something as clear as unfiltered Grade C).

"So Robert," I said, mustering an evaporator-full of reverence. "How much syrup you make this year?"

"Oh...'nough to feed my family," he muttered. I realized that was one of "those" questions.

"Uh...how many taps did you put out this year?" I went on, knowing better.

"Welllllll...don't know that I know," he said, like every word caused him severe pain. "Gosh," he went on, "you know...the numbers're liable [pronounced *larble*] to change from year to year."

Suddenly I knew how deep the Fairfield Dodge is ingrained and that neither God nor Mike Wallace could coax answers out of sugarmaker Robert! I bade him farewell and resumed my stroll through the Festival's midway.

Howrigan is a famous Fairfield surname and I'm honored to know many of the Howrigans. Francis Howrigan was a great friend, sugarmaker, and businessman. In his prime he gathered from over 10,000 buckets and milked a hundred head of cows, all while maintaining a legendary image as Franklin County senator. His son, Raymond, took over the farm operation just before Francis passed away and, with the help of his three boys, has modernized it and built a new sugarhouse. Back when Francis was still in charge, Vermont had one of those sugar seasons where the warm, sunny weather begat nothing but dark syrup. There was a desperate drought of light amber that year and rumors were rampant that Francis Howrigan had dug a hole and buried a huge surplus of drums of Fancy the previous year. Those who tried to buy that cached syrup were treated with an abridged version of the Fairfield Dodge, however: Frances just chuckled and walked away. Raymond and his boys visited my sugarhouse a few weeks ago and I saw my chance to have some fun with Raymond.

"Any truth to that rumor about your dad burying all that Fancy syrup?" I asked.

Raymond went instinctively into Dodge mode : "Gosh...you never know what a fella's going to do," he said, but the folds of his scrunched up face failed to hide a grin.

I met sugarmakers from all over the maple world at the festival that day and learned, once again, what great folks they are. I don't suppose we'll ever learn if there's liquid gold buried in them thar Fairfield hills but it doesn't matter. Traditions are what matter. The Vermont Maple Festival has been a tradition for forty years and counting. It's a great chance for maple folks to compare notes, tout their wares, and give a sampling of their syrup. It's also a chance for layfolks to meet maple professionals for lots of sweet talk...or not.

Chapter 61

Two Breaths of Spring

WE HAVE TWO SPRING SEASONS here in Vermont. The first is, of course, our sweet and famous maple sugarin'. Sugarin's part of my genetic makeup so, you see, it's not income or livelihood that leads me to the woods every spring but something instinctive and unforgiving. Just as a squirrel gathers nuts or a dog waters hydrants, when spring comes I've gotta sugar, rain or shine, feast or famine, or more appropriately, snow or snow. Speaking of snow, this year Saint Valentine greeted us with thirty-six inches of the stuff, three dozen ways to say "I love you!" The day after that holiday dumping, I would rather have skipped sugarin' altogether but I proceeded with deep, snowshoe-trudging steps toward the season ahead. This may come as a surprise, since on the outside I look like a happy-go-lucky sugarmaker, but the rigidness of "having to do it" sometimes creates negatives in my sugar-making life; no drop in the bucket for a happy-go-lucky sugarmaker.

Sugarin' used to entail working our woolen-clad butts off hanging 3,000 buckets and then waiting for the freezing nights and thawing days to fill 'em up. Modern sugarin' can find the preseason even more difficult than buckets though. When sap starts running, plastic tubing is no help at all unless it's tight, free of leaks, and above the snow. This year all of the above were problems in addition to another piece of modern sugarin' called vacuum. Vacuum allows us to milk the trees like milking cows, only our maple milk house covers a hundred acres and requires ten miles of piping. My son Tommy did an excellent job of installing two new vacuum pumps, but our ten miles of aged piping created more problems than you could shake a sap yoke at. The vacuum experts said our new pumps should deliver twenty-two inches of mercury way back in the woods. "Inches of mercury, indeed," I huffed—seems to me mercury should be measured in leaps and bounds, or miles per hour, but never inches! Since the best reading we ever got was fifteen inches, our sugar season found this aging Vermonter, his son, and several others searching, in leaps and bounds, for an elusive seven inches of something invisible to the human eye and devil-ishly unpredictable—vacuum.

My frustration peaked one day when an elderly man came to visit. It was just before noon and I was in the sugarhouse getting ready for the season's first boil. He found me grumbling about one of the multi-problems that always accompany the first boil, walked up to me, and placed his hand on my shoulder. He noted that I looked like I carried the weight of the world on those shoulders. Among the other soothing words he used, I remember him saying "...after all, Burr, the ceiling's not falling in." His kind words helped and after he left, I walked home for a quick lunch. I was so encour-aged by my new frame of mind that I hardly noticed the pile of ragged insulation and torn sheetrock lying outside the kitchen door. As I entered, Betsy stood stricken-looking under a gaping hole by the refrigerator—the kitchen ceiling had fallen in!

We finished cleaning up from our very trying sugar season the other day and as I came home for another quick lunch, a carpenter had just picked up his tools from rebuilding our kitchen ceiling. A much happier Betsy had prepared me a sandwich and as I sat down to eat it, I asked her for ideas on my next newsletter. She pointed outside to the lilacs that line our walkway and said, "I asked your father once what his favorite season was, thinking he'd say sugarin'. He surprised me—said 'blossom time'." Harry Morse loved the period after sugarin' ends, when the Vermont countryside bursts with a luscious greenness and the lilac bushes and apple trees provide our second spring season— "blossom time." I stepped out and stretched a clump of purple lilac blossoms to my nose. Its wonderful aroma stirred my nostalgia toward pleasant, easy times in my life—end of school, family pic-nics, summer's promises. I knew right then that I had to honor this glorious season in writing, even at the expense of our precious maple sugarin'.

Where sugarin's hard labor and stress somehow translates to a mys-tique that's part of our Vermont being, blossom season comes with no strings attached—an unconditional gift. Our farm hosts numerous ancient apple trees and lilacs, standing guardians to abandoned cellar holes. Sure, someone originally planted them but they require none of the attention that their cousins, the roses and azaleas, do. They seem to grow forever and each spring, for a breath of time, put on a show that equals a whole season—blossom season.

It seems the whole world has maple sugarin' on its mind from February to June: in February folks want to know how the season's going to be and in

June they want to know how it was. The next time I answer that proverbial question with the words "sweet, fragrant, and world-class," with all apologies to you maple romantics out there, I won't necessarily be thinking of sugarin'.

Chapter 62

The Wonders of Fall

WITH THE FANTASTIC SHOW our foliage is putting on, it's impossible to ignore the beauty around us these days. We here in Vermont are able to bank on this brilliance with our trust in Mother Nature and also, quite literally, with the surety that folks will come from all over the world to see the vibrant color. Another thing we can bank on is that, with that huge onslaught of humanity, there will be a few folks who really stand out. I'm going to dedicate this column to that group...those who showed a personality as vivid as the leaves and left my mouth agape.

One day a group of Englishmen came in the sugarhouse. English people are always a hit for me because we share common humor genes. In my presentation I make reference to the taste of maple sap. I say it tastes much like water and I drink it right out of the bucket, not for any nutritional value but to quench my thirst. At that point I remove my cap, bare my bald pate and say, "It doesn't do a damned thing for the hairline." They all laugh and to milk the line even more, I pick out a bald man in the crowd, look squarely at him, and say, "It almost looks like a SAP drinker came right along with your group today." The man I pick usually gets red in the face and chuckles, pleased with the gag. The man I picked that day, however, sat stone-faced, except for a slight elevation of his aristocratic-looking nose. I knew I had blown it with him and when he approached me at the end of my show, I prepared for a royal lambasting. Close up, he looked even more stuffy than he had from a distance. He spoke with a stiff tone, much like he had just discovered dog poop in his prize rose bush. "Sir, I would shake your hand but I am certain that it would be STICKY!" With that he about-faced and went directly to his bus, satisfied that my brazenness had been checked.

Another man was the opposite of stuffy. His group had just been to Graniteville, an area pocked with giant cavities in the earth and mountains of granite waste. We Vermonters think of the granite quarries as age-old but their relative newness mystified that man. After my show, he approached me with puzzlement that looked like it had been sewn into his face.

"Awh know how long these parts been populated with them Native 'Mericans an' all that. When they tole us over t' quarries that granite had been mined for oney a couple hunnert year it just 'bout blowed my mind...awh mean look at them Gyptians over there n' KAY-ro...they was buildin' them PERmids a thousand year ago! Awh says to m'seff, with all that granite, you should have the biggest PERmids in th' worl rite cheer in VERmont!"

I told him that I'd never thought of that (and although my mind's pretty darned active, I surely never had), and agreed with him that it was a consideration. My eyes followed him leaving the sugarhouse, and later, boarding his bus; it may be my imagination but I swear his head still shook with disbelief about what didn't occur in these Green Mountains way back in 2560 BC!

My cutest visitor was a small girl from Georgia. I was in between buses and noticed her family exiting our Woodshed Theatre. All of a sudden the girl, who looked to be about eight, exclaimed, "That's Mr. Burr, the man on the brochure." Although I craved a break from incessant maple questions, and felt especially weary of youngsters, I couldn't ignore recognition like that. The girl's mother approached me and explained that, somewhere down the road, she had let her daughter, Emili, vote on going to the Teddy Bear Factory or the maple farm. When she said that Emili had voted to see sap buckets at the maple farm, my heart melted. "Wow," I thought. "This is some dynamic young lady!"

I carefully explained that it was the wrong time of year to see sap buckets, but walked her and her family through an explanation of the whole process right there in my sugarhouse. Emili listened like an adult and afterward took numerous pictures with a pint-sized camera. Just before they left, I handed her a tiny sap-spout lucky charm that had been given to me. "But maybe your good luck will go away now, Mr. Burr," she suggested. "Not to worry, young lady," I said, thinking of being visited by an eight-year-old girl who would rather see sap buckets than teddy bears.." I'm the luckiest guy in the world."

We have reached our peak color at the close of this writing and soon both leaves and tourists will depart. For a time, I allowed my thoughts to be scattered like the leaves. I thought of the world's biggest pyramids looming on the horizon south of our farm and maple trees supporting full sap buckets year-round. "Hmmm...it would be great for the cash flow," I thought. Then, suddenly my mind snapped back to reality and I knew I'd vote for the four seasons over all the money in the world.

Part Four

Miracle of Music

Chapter 63

Digital Doldrums

IT SEEMS THE FICKLE FINGER of fate has mapped out a fingerless world for me, so to speak. I started thinking about fingers this morning when I listened to a conversation on National Public Radio with a guy who wrote a book on typewriters—remember...those things from the olden days? This guy said there are several theories on why the letters were placed the way they were on the keyboard. One that fascinated me was that all the letters to spell "typewriter" appear on the top line, a handy gimmick for non-typing salesmen to fake speed. The theory that I believe, however, is that an alphabetical placement allowed the typist to type too fast for the mechanical components of the machine to handle—they mixed up the letters to slow the typist down! I've always admired folks who could pound away at a keyboard, like my sister Susie. In her time, she's threatened many a typewriter with meltdown and still threatens the business end of computers the same way. Fingers are wonderful appendages, but only if you can chew bubble gum and ride a bike at the same time—I can't.

I wanted to learn typing when I was a kid but was denied that right by a principal back in Montpelier High School. One day, I went into his office requesting a change in my schedule that would allow typing class. The balding, portly man sat, fixed on some paperwork in front of him, and motioned to a classroom chair at the edge of his huge steel desk. It seemed like an eternity before he looked up but when he did, it was with kind eyes.

"You're one of the Morses from the County Road aren't you?...know your Uncle Ira."

"Yes sir," I replied.

"So you want to take typing...I'm not sure about that...let me see your hands," he said, rising up in his chair for a more direct look. I placed ten fat, stubby fingers on his desk, feeling a little embarrassed. He pondered for a minute, put his fingers together in the shape of a tent, and spoke: "Harry [he used my real name], you have the hands of a farmer. Morses are farmers. Why don't we set you up with a course that'll prepare you for Ag school...typing won't help you." Thoughts of my heritage and the fifty cows that awaited my role in the evening's milking came flooding over me. I glanced at the framed certificate hanging on his wall with the words "Doctor of Philosophy" just above his own name, Robert T. Chastney. "He must know," I thought, my young mind failing at even a feeblest attempt at argument. He reached to shake my farmer's hand as I rose from my chair and thanked him. I walked back into the hallways that would eventually lead me to Ag school, never telling him that I wanted to be a writer.

Music also played into my fingerless future. Sometime before the incident with Dr. Chastney, I took piano lessons from my Aunt June. She was a wonderful teacher and praised me for my good ear and ability to pick tunes out of my head. The translation of those tunes onto a piano keyboard, however, never worked that well with my bumbling digits. One day, after a particularly bad lesson, I decided to walk away from piano lessons. June Morse was the best teacher a kid could ever have, but the one variable on the road to piano proficiency I could not accept was proper fingering. Years later, I came home one night $125 poorer with a beautiful blond...a blond-colored Kay Bass violin, that is! I've always been fascinated by the subtle but so important role an upright bass plays in jazz and wanted to be one of those guys with the fondling stance and the plucking fingers. Alas, however, after a couple years doomed by the digits, I gave up the bass. It's been thirty-seven years since I graduated from Ag school and I've spent the interim right here on this farm. I love my life and appreciate the old principal for trying to tweak my fate. Fate, however, scorns tweaking even from Ph.Ds. Yes, I've honored my heritage by being a farmer all these years but have never closed the door on life's residuals.

Soon after the bass episode, I made up my mind to hone my talents on the one instrument that seemed within my grasp, the slide trombone. I play my horn about every day, no fingering needed. One of fate's most recent turns has led me to, yes, the world of writing. As I sit here pounding out column # 141 my two-fingered way, I wonder if typing class would have been good for me...guess I'll never know.

Chapter 64

Friends for Life

A LOT OF CHARACTERS have worked on the Morse Farm over the years, like the old guy who wore a three-cornered hat and thought he was Napoleon and the young man who drove his 1957 Mercury everywhere in reverse, except when he wanted to back up—then he'd "slip her right into drive!" Yup, we've had some characters, but none stands out in my memory more than my buddy, Chuck Parker. Chuck and I went through high school, college, and into the 40th Army Band together. I don't know why we should have become such good buddies; I mean he was a big, Type A guy who came on like a bulldozer and got girls by the dozen. I was a pudgy, Grade C kid with a Rodney Dangerfield attitude.

We were in the same gym class as freshmen at Montpelier High School in 1962. I stood in the huge gymnasium on the first day of classes, no doubt pondering how many hay bales could be stored there, when a big kid walked up and slugged me in the shoulder.

"Hey Morse—I'm Parker. My father's going to arrange for me to work at your farm this summer." He loomed a full head taller than me and I figured he must be trying to pick a fight. "Not if I get a say in the matter," I thought. I was fresh from eight grades in East Montpelier one-room schools and scared to death of this kid Parker and his big city school. He went on, "Really Morse—you can teach me how to drive a tractor and stuff like that." He had my attention with that one—suggesting that there was something I could do better than him.

Chuck Parker was in a couple of my other classes plus band where, as a tuba player, he sat close to me in the trombone section. With time I learned that he really wasn't trying to pick a fight and accepted him as an ally. I often asked his advice on two foreign and terrifying subjects, mathematics and girls, and his continual quizzing about farm stuff made me feel good for something. By the time school ended in June, we were good friends and when he started work on the farm, I was excited to have him there.

He worked well for a city kid, probably because of his Mount Holly, Vermont, ancestry; his father, Gilbert, grew up on a Mount Holly side-hill farm that was even more ornery than our farm. Chuck, I suppose, gained certain farm protocol through osmosis, like Thou shalt not smoke in the barn, (or in my case, Thou shalt not smoke, period!). One time Chuck and I were standing just outside our hay barn sharing a smoke when I suddenly saw my father heading our way. I handed the cigarette off to Chuck and he camouflaged it quicker than you could say "LSMFT." My father walked up, tipped his cap, and said in his quiet, even tone, "Chuck—your pocket seems to be on fire.".

Haying back in those days seemed to go on forever. Chuck and I hefted bales till our fingers were raw and I remember many trips from the huge hayfield on the western side of our farm to our hay barn. On that route was a bricked-up spring we'd stop at for cold water. A tin ladle hung at the spring's edge on an apple tree, but usually we'd get down on our knees and scoop the cold water onto our faces with our hands and drink from our cupped palms. One stifling hot day, I was down in that prayerful position when Chuck said, "Morse, reach down deeper where the coldest water is." I plunged my arms further in and there, close to the bottom, my right hand formed around an object that would become all too familiar to us that summer—a bottle of Genesee beer. Chuck had planted a six-pack there earlier and thus began our greater bonding, illegal as it was, as drinking buddies.

Chuck Parker eventually went on to make a big mark in Kansas City as the CEO of a national company that sells meat-processing equipment. My brother, Tick, has occasionally worked for Chuck's company building electronic controls. He recently told of an interesting phone call with Chuck. He said there was a rustling noise in the background as they discussed the particulars of a project. It seems Chuck was also working with glue as he talked on the phone. "Time's too precious to just talk—you gotta also be doin' something with your hands," Chuck had always claimed. My brother said Chuck seemed distracted as their conversation wound down. When Tick asked if everything was all right, he learned that Charles R. Parker, corporate guru and international traveler, had glued his fingers together!

Thinking of where our lives have led us brings me back to the MHS gymnasium. At the risk of sounding unglued, I'll say that, in a big way, our lives haven't changed much. Sure, he's gone on to corporate America and I've stayed here and brought Morse Farm to new levels but, thanks to God, we're both alive, well, and growing old. Underneath all the glitter, our personalities are still the same old Type A and Grade C. We've remained friends all these years and helped each other along the way (he even loaned me his sister, who's been my wife now for some thirty years). In fact, if it weren't for the distance between Montpelier and Kansas City, we might be reaching for a cold Genesee right now to toast our lifetime friendship.

Chapter 65

Lake George or Bust

I WAS FEELING A BIT extravagant, sheepish in fact, as I headed out last Saturday morning to fill in with the St. Johnsbury Concert Band at a band festival in Lake George, New York. As luck would have it, I had a book signing in Poultney, Vermont, later that same day. Being a Vermonter, pleasure always comes easier when I can couple it with a little business! The day was sunny as I headed south on I-89. I was excited to be playing with the St Johnsbury group, the third oldest band in the country. The band's director, Gary Aubin, is a multi-generation Vermonter and showed typical Vermont aloofness when I asked for specific directions: "Just go that way and you'll find it." He pointed west! I was beginning to look forward to my day when sprinkles first appeared in Bethel, just thirty miles from home. "Good thing I'm headed west, away from the rain," I thought, putting the wipers on slow speed. The sprinkles, however, had another plan. By the time I reached Rutland, my wipers were on high speed and so were my feelings of gloom. In view of Gary's directions, I had not even broached the subject of rain locations or possible cancellations.

My passage into New York State lacked the excitement I usually feel at that point in a trip. In fact, that day it brought only a dreary upgrade from heavy rain to torrential downpour. I could just barely make out the landmarks, distinguished by flatter land and billboards. We Vermonters are a bit smug in our billboardless state but I found myself pondering them through the downpour, wishing they could lead me directly to the exact location of the Lake George Band Festival. They went, however, from the useless to the ridiculous: Hook, Line & Snookerd, Law Office, Let Us Help You Sue Someone. I finally turned right at a sign that promised Lake George somewhere that-a-way. It was a route that wound through a hilly part of New York. Muddy freshets rushed from the steep banks onto the road ahead.

Finally the lake itself appeared, suggesting there would also be a village of the same name up ahead. I was about to stop and ask directions (another thing native Vermonters don't usually do) when a sign introduced Lake George Village. It said, Population 933— a figure that grossly conflicted with the mishmash of fast food places and convenience stores on the main thoroughfare. "Typical," I thought. "Nine hundred thirty-three residents and thirty thousand tourists on a summer day!" The road was flooded in places. Several cars sat stranded in door-deep water and I was being very careful to not join those ranks. Since time was running short, I stopped at a convenience store by the village park. The man behind the counter answered my query with a gruff, smoker's voice.

"Da ban thing? Yea...it's sposa be in Shepard's Park rightchair." He pointed just beyond my parked car. "Think it's history, though, Pal. You know, da rain an such."

I thanked him and sprinted toward Shepard's Park. On a nice day the lakeside amphitheater would have been a perfect place for a band concert, but that day it stood stark and empty, except for four people who congregated midstage. From a distance they looked ragged and their movements were awkward. As I reached them, I could see that they were four guys whose fishing had been rained out. They were very drunk. They looked toward me as if I was the one doing weird things. I must have looked weird, in fact, with my white shirt and black pants drenched from the pouring rain. One of them approached me with a beer crudely concealed in his shirt.

"Havabeerman," he slurred, grinning like a fool.

"No, I can't...really...I'm in a hurry...do you guys know where that band event is?"

"Ban e venn? Oh yah got moved t' th' high schhhhhhoool."

They proceeded to give me group directions that involved lots of back slapping, traffic light counting and pointing in all directions. I thanked them and followed the most reasonable of their directions, reaching the high school five minutes before our downbeat. The rest of the St. Johnsbury group had arrived early. They welcomed me, their trombone ringer, as we filed into a large gymnasium. I settled into the third trombone chair, cringing at the feeling of soaked clothing against dry chair. Needless to say, the uniqueness went beyond playing in America's third oldest band.

After we finished playing, I made the short drive to Poultney, Vermont, and my book signing. I sold more books than I expected, possibly because of folks looking for indoor things to do. It was still pouring when I headed home at 9 p.m. As I drove north through the stretch of woods between Rutland and Bethel, the humor of the day finally caught up with me. I laughed out loud about the four drunks—"Maybe I should have stayed with them," I thought! The rain stopped at exactly the same place it had started ten hours earlier, lending another layer of suspense to my life. As I walked into my house that night, the air was crisp and clean, like an encore to a perfect day. You know, the more I think it over, it was a perfect day: along with some good clean business, it also delivered a story and a song— it really can't get any better than that.

Epilogue

BY THOMAS MORSE

I consider myself inherently lucky to have grown up on our ancestral farm in a beautiful place like East Montpelier, Vermont. My paternal grandparents were our neighbors and the rest of my dad's family was scattered around the farm. This is something most kids don't get to experience. I grew up surrounded by acres of pristine farm fields and forestland to explore. This, and the presence of our prosperous country store run by my parents and grandparents made my childhood idyllic in a way I believe is becoming rare in our increasingly fast paced, urbanized society. In my opinion, family farming enterprises harken back to simpler times, when land and ways of life were routinely passed along from generation to generation.

While our family has been making maple syrup for two hundred years now, it wasn't until my father was out of agricultural college that sugaring became the focal point of the business. Along with being an ingenious farmer, my grandfather, Harry Morse, Sr., had remarkable foresight and realized early on that Vermont's signature product was its maple syrup. Tired of the drudgery (and shrinking profit margins) of dairy farming, he decided he would try to create a year-round business based primarily around selling maple products. Needing a good partner, he asked his youngest son, my father, Harry Jr., or Burr as everyone knows him, to join him in this vision. My dad accepted the offer, and father and son, starting from scratch, went on to carve out a remarkable worldwide niche for their business right here on the home farm. Like many of the most successful entrepreneurial operations, they started off small—very small. Over the course of forty years, their seasonal, roadside produce and syrup stand has become one of the premier tourist destinations in the state of Vermont.

I came along somewhere in the middle of this amazing evolution. The business I remember as a small child was a much humbler version of what it is today. The store building was less than half its current size and I'm sure gross sales back then mirrored this ratio. Maple had become the bread and butter for the business, but summertime was still all about growing a bounty of vegetable and fruit crops. My grandparents had a lifelong obsession for propagating any of God's abundant flora that they could on our farm. From Christmas trees to perennial flowers to root crops and berries to the lily pads in their pond, there wasn't much that Harry and Dot Morse did not try their hand at growing at one point or another. The law of diminishing returns when it came to growing produce in our farm's stony, clay-based soil was hardly a deterrent for them. Although my father was always more concerned about the business's bottom line than his free-spirited parents, he shared their love for all things green, and the three of them worked tirelessly in the fields all summer long.

Consequently, my brother Rob and I grew up spending the first several weeks of summer vacation with Mom and Dad, on our hands and knees picking strawberries for twenty-five cents a quart. The rest of our summer was spent weeding the next year's crop of berries, as well as tending to and harvesting raspberries, blueberries, sweet corn, and pumpkins as well as hot-packing huge amounts of maple syrup for the autumn tourist rush. From this, I gained not only a strong work ethic at a young age, but also the knowledge that the harder I worked, the more I myself, and the farm as a whole, would profit in the long run. This was an invaluable lesson and one that any aspiring small business owner (especially us farmers) needs to fully appreciate.

As enjoyable as the dog days of summer and the thrill of foliage season with our booming tourist trade were as a kid on the farm, it was springtime and specifically our sugaring operation that got my blood pumping the fastest. Sugaring time was a magical time for us boys. Before we were old enough to help much with the incredible workload that defines our industry, we were underfoot in the sugarhouse and hanging from the sides of the sap-gathering rig as it bounced down the road. We learned the trade as it should be, from our father and from both of our grandfathers. My mother's father, Gil Parker, grew up producing syrup on his family's southern Vermont farm and loved to lend a hand to our operation. Sugaring was truly in our blood and we relished the springtime with its wet snowstorms, knee-deep mud holes, and days when the sap seemed to fill our collection tanks as fast as we could gather it in.

Sugaring, like everything else on our farm, has evolved greatly in my lifetime. The basics are still the same—we even use the same arch and flue pan that we had when I was a kid. The intricacies of collecting the sap and boiling it down, however, have changed a lot. Some of these changes, or improvements one might say, were born of the natural human inclination to make things easier and more streamlined. Others, however, came about due to pure necessity. They say that necessity is the mother of invention and nowhere is this truer than in the maple industry where we depend on exacting weather conditions that seem to get a little less dependable with each passing season. The pure and simple fact is that in my relatively short life (twenty-seven years and counting), our climate here in north central Vermont has changed a great deal. This has, most certainly, negatively impacted our operation as well as the local sugaring industry as a whole.

When I was a kid, we could count on several weeks' worth of prime "sap weather" every spring, when cold, crisp nights would give way to bright sunny days. With temperatures rising to around forty-three degrees and winds out of the west, the sap run started early and would soon be more than we could handle. I'd go on a gathering run with my Grandpa Gil, "Bopa" as we called him, and find most of our tanks running over. Oftentimes, we'd get a week straight of these ideal conditions and we'd be producing syrup nearly around the clock. These tremendous sap runs of my youth have taken on an almost mythical quality to me in light of the poor production we have seen in recent years. I remember wishing aloud to my dad before the start of this past season that we would have enough sap to boil all night long at least once. Guess what? I'm still wishing. Being a sugarmaker these days is a little like being a Red Sox fan was before the '04 season—our favorite phrase has become "There's always next year!" Today, we might get a handful of these optimum days every spring. The rest of the season we are dependent on vacuum pumps and airtight pipeline systems to provide us with sap on days when Mother Nature (and gravity) would rather not. We had no vacuum pumps when I was young. Instead, we depended solely on loose, aged tubing, nature's good graces, and Sir Isaac Newton's laws of gravity to provide us our sap. We were rarely disappointed.

As sugarmakers today, we are working year-round to maintain and develop our sap delivery system. This is now proven to be the deciding factor in any sugaring operations' ultimate success. In those bygone days of my youth, with sagging, squirrel-chewed tubing systems, and no vacuum, we'd get more sap than all of our fancy equipment is yielding today! While incredibly frustrating, this truly illustrates how quickly our climate is changing. Kind of scary, I'd say. Instead of throwing in the towel, however, we're forging ahead, expanding our operations and striving to improve our already intricate tubing network. After all, sugaring is an addiction for us, and quitting would be akin to selling off the farm piece by piece to the highest bidder. More precisely, it's what Harry would have wanted.

It might have been a young boy's imagination, but I swear that today, even when weather conditions are perfect, sap just doesn't seem to gush out of a mainline like I remember as a kid. In any event, every year we struggle, (with more taps and tens of thousands of dollars invested in new equipment), to make the eight to nine hundred gallons of syrup we took for granted back in the good ole' days. As they say, things ain't what they used to be.

My fondest childhood sugaring memories include watching Dad and Grampa Harry working together in the sugarhouse, boiling up a storm, endlessly firing the arch and drawing off syrup, sometimes one hundred gallons in one day. When I was around ten, Harry had a series of debilitating strokes that eventually landed him in a wheelchair. As a result, my early memories of him and Dad working side by side in the sugarhouse are some of the ones I cherish the most.

In those days we were still burning four-foot cordwood—forty cords a season to be exact. All of this was wood that my father, grandfather, and some hired hands processed constantly in the off season. Today we burn hardwood chips that are delivered on a tractor trailer—"better than buying oil from the Arabs!" my incorrigible grandfather would undoubtedly say. Rob and I would fill a dolly (that had stake sides that were taller than I was) with several hundred pounds of softwood slabs and dried hardwood and push it along a track out of the woodshed and to the front of the arch. Dad would open the often red-hot iron doors, agitate the wickedly hot fire with a long poker, and then rapidly throw half the wood we'd just brought him into the firebox. He'd shut the doors with his poker quickly to maintain the burning consistency that we now get automatically with our wood-chip gasifier. I've never seen anyone who works with more efficiency and swiftness than my father. As a kid, watching Dad and Gramp expertly tend the huge evaporator was a magnificent experience for me

For supper, Gramp would drop some hot dogs into the far compartment of the syrup pan and let them boil for a few minutes. After a long day of gathering sap and filling the wood cart, nothing could have tasted any better than one of Grampa Harry's sap hot dogs! Since then, that particular tradition has ceased. Undoubtedly, a large portion of our clientele would probably not appreciate the campyness of our dinner franks cooking in their maple syrup.

After supper, Mom would come down from the house to get Rob and me. She literally had to drag us out of that sugarhouse. The thought of Dad boiling late into the night without us was excruciating. And all so that we could wake up and go to school! How disgusting. Our real education, we decided early on, occurred right there in the sugarhouse, under the watchful tutelage of our father and grandfather.

I have a lasting memory of Rob and me ritualistically peering down at the sugarhouse from our bedroom window before falling asleep. After our eyes adjusted, the dark silhouette of the old building would appear, with gaps between its boards through which we could glimpse light and steam. It was never long before a bright shower of sparks would come flying out of the stack. That signaled to us that Dad or Grampa was firing the arch with some flashy softwood slabs from our neighbor's sawmill. Suddenly the night was aglow, and with it, the hearts of two little boys who treasured their family's age-old tradition.